The Battle of Bunker Hill

*A novella based upon the docudrama
"The Battle of Bunker Hill"
by* **William R. Chemerka**

The Battle of Bunker Hill: A Novella based upon the Docudrama
© 2013 William R. Chemerka. All Rights Reserved.

No part of this book may be reproduced in any form or by any means, electronic, mechanical, digital, photocopying or recording, except for the inclusion in a review, without permission in writing from the publisher.

Published in the USA by:
BearManor Media
PO Box 1129
Duncan, Oklahoma 73534-1129
www.bearmanormedia.com

ISBN 978-1-59393-270-1

Printed in the United States of America.
Book design by Brian Pearce | Red Jacket Press.

To Sumner C. Putnam, a descendant of General Israel Putnam

Table of Contents

Acknowledgments 7
Introduction 9
The Debate at Hartwell's Tavern 11
The Morgan Farm 17
A Father and Son 21
General Israel Putnam 25
The Ride of Joseph Rodgers 27
The March to Charlestown Neck 31
Building the Defenses 37
General Gage's Plan 45
The Thunder of British Artillery 49
Crossing the Charles River 53
The First Attack 57
A Mother's Prayer 63
The Second Attack 65
The Final Attack 69
Young Soldiers 73
Bayonets Against Fists 75
A Costly Victory 79
Epilogue 81
Photo Section 83
Appendix A: Causes of the American Revolution 91
Appendix B: Historical Notes 95
Appendix C: Cast and Crew 97
Appendix D: DVD Docudrama and Historical Perspective 101
Appendix E: DVD Special Features 103

Acknowledgments

Thanks to Tony Malanowski for his original story idea, the first in his history series "America: Her People, Her Stories." Tony was the producer and director of *The Battle of Bunker Hill* and served in other important post-production positions. For more information, go to *www.bunkerhilldvd.com*.

A special salute to the cast, crew, and historical interpreters who helped bring *The Battle of Bunker Hill* to life! Also thanks to all those who allowed the production team to film on their property, especially the staff at the Howell Living History Farm, a facility of the Mercer County, New Jersey, Park Commission, where the main Bunker Hill exterior fortifications were constructed.

Thanks again to Ben Ohmart, Sandra Grabman, Michelle Morgan, Jessie Fries, Brian Pearce, and the rest of the staff at BearManor Media for all their creative help and support.

Introduction

It is the morning of June 17, 1775.

The previous night, under the cover of darkness, colonial patriots had quickly constructed an impromptu fortification on Breed's Hill across the harbor from Boston. They now await a full assault by the King's soldiers — the best equipped and most feared fighting force in the world.

These colonists have little ammunition or water, but on this hot summer morning, they will stand as one against the mighty British infantry…relying on something which they have in abundance: courage. And by the end of the day, the world would know whether this ragged band of farmers, merchants, and shopkeepers — the colonial militia — would be able to help bring a new nation into being.

The Battle of Bunker Hill is the story of the first major military conflict of the American Revolution and how two fathers and two sons left their respective farms to defend the heights overlooking Boston.

This novella provides more details about the characters — both historical and fictional — that appeared in the 2009 production. And it introduces readers to several characters that did not appear in the completed docudrama.

William R. Chemerka

PART ONE

The Debate at Hartwell's Tavern

"It <u>will</u> be a fight for freedom!"

It had been a bloody April in Massachusetts.

On the morning of April 19, 1775, armed colonists were fired upon by British regulars on Lexington Green. Hours later at Concord, colonial militias attacked the soldiers. The retreating Redcoats were fired upon during their march back to Boston. By nightfall, over one hundred colonists and soldiers had been killed and over two hundred more had been wounded. The American Revolution had begun.

Ephraim Hartwell's tavern in Lincoln stood on the road between Lexington and Concord, where the combat had been especially intense. The wooden walls of the building even bore splintered scars from musket balls that had been fired during the fighting. The tavern was more than a place that served good food and drink: it was the principal gathering place — other than the church — for the men of the area. It was in the tavern, around the clustered oak tables and amidst the candlelight and tobacco smoke from dozens of clay pipes at night, where the news of the day was discussed and debated.

"Can you still believe it happened?" asked Joseph Rodgers, the tall, silver-haired book binder. "The King's own soldiers killing his subjects."

"*Subjects?*" questioned Thomas Hadley bitterly. "They killed my *cousin* — my cousin, Samuel, on Lexington Green. And they'll pay for that!"

"They've already paid, Thomas, and then some, on the road back from Concord!" said Edmund Bateman, a veteran of the French and Indian War whose left ear had been sliced in half by an arrow. "We filled those lobsterbacks with lead, eh, lads?"

"That we did, Edmund," replied John Hartwell, whose father owned the tavern. John Hartwell served in a minuteman company, a militia unit that was designed to respond first to any alarm or threat. The colonial militia units formed each month on town greens and conducted musket drills under the command of an elected officer. During the French and Indian War, the drills were serious events, but after the peace treaty was signed in 1763, the military gatherings became more like social events. On more than one occasion, conversation and laughter replaced marching in ranks. However, since the passage of the Intolerable Acts, which closed Boston Harbor to trade and placed restrictions on town meetings, the monthly drills became solemn affairs again.

"And we'll do it again, if need be!" shouted Isaac Hartwell, John's brother, from a nearby table. "That we will, my friends, and with Providence on our side!"

A brief cheer erupted as tankards and mugs of ale clashed against each other. But a few of the men sat silently; not everyone was in favor of armed conflict with Great Britain.

"They tried to make us pay the tax on tea, but what a party we had that night in Boston," continued Bateman, as if he were delivering a sermon. "They closed the harbor, revoked our charter, and tried to disarm us on Lexington Green. And we showed 'em good, by God! And now we've got 'em cornered like harbor rats in Boston."

Again, some of the men cheered. Bateman held his drink in the air. Others tapped their tankards together and toasted each other.

"Most importantly, we must know who is with us and who is not!" exclaimed Hadley.

"Aye!" shouted Bateman in agreement.

Ephraim Hartwell emerged from the kitchen with a large plate of roasted chicken, ham, and potatoes. "Enough of this talk for now," said the elder Hartwell as he shuffled across the wooden floor and placed the plate on Isaac's table. "'Tis time to eat."

"And drink!" added John Hartwell. "More rum for me!" The men clanked their mugs together in yet another toast. Ned Carpenter, a young man of eighteen who worked in the tavern, quickly walked over to the tables and filled the men's empty mugs with ale.

For several minutes, the sounds of eating and drinking replaced the political and military conversations. The entire atmosphere of the tavern recalled happier times. But that soon changed.

"I say this," said Ebeneezer Wilcox, a local wheelwright who did not join in the cheerful toasts. "The bloodshed should not prevent us from settling our differences peacefully."

"'Tis not peace that will settle this, Ebeneezer," replied Hadley, who frowned at Wilcox's remarks.

"Aye," said Rodgers. "More lead and powder will."

More tankards were hoisted amidst a verbal volley of "Ayes!"

When the clamoring eased, William Morgan, a rugged forty-five-year-old farmer who sat alone at a nearby table, looked Rodgers in the eyes.

"The cat's got your tongue, eh?" smiled Rodgers. "Come, sit with us, Will."

Morgan rose and walked over to Rodgers' table.

"Well, Will, what do you think?" asked Rodgers.

"Is my opinion that important?" quipped Morgan.

"Indeed," replied Rodgers.

Morgan took a sip of ale from his cow horn cup and wiped his mouth. "He may be right," he noted.

"Aye, Will," replied Rodgers. "Hadley makes sense, although he's had a bit too much to drink again."

"No, not Hadley," corrected Morgan. "Wilcox."

A quick silence came over the group who sat nearby. The quietness quickly spread throughout Hartwell's. Morgan, an infrequent visitor to the tavern, rarely spoke of politics; he preferred to listen. But when he spoke, he chose his words wisely. He was well respected in the community as a man of determination and common sense.

"What the King's troops did was wrong, a tragic wrong," said Morgan as several men turned their chairs and faced him. "And, yes, they paid a price: a terrible price in blood. General Gage's soldiers once roamed freely over this land, but now his troops are confined to Boston, surrounded by our militia camps. But now is...."

"And why aren't you there right now?" interrupted Hadley.

"Because I'm *here*, you drunken fool," said Morgan.

The men laughed.

"Will and I were on picket duty last night with Captain Josephson," said Rodgers. "You know that, Thomas."

"But that was *last* night," said Hadley. "Tonight, he sounds as if he's still loyal to his King." Hadley turned to Morgan, who took another sip of ale from his cup. Then Morgan looked away, ignoring Hadley.

"Never debate a man full of ale, eh, Will?" chuckled Rodgers. Bateman rose up from his chair and looked at Morgan. "I'm sober, so I'll repeat the question," he said firmly. "So, just who do you serve, William Morgan?"

A brief silence filled the smoky room.

"I serve no one," said Morgan.

Some of the men seemed uncomfortable with his reply.

"You have no loyalties, sir, no responsibilities?" questioned Bateman.

"I provide for myself, my wife, and my children," replied Morgan. "Those responsibilities occupy me enough."

Bateman finished his drink and walked away from Morgan. He paused near another table. "We must take action against the Crown," stated Bateman. "And in our efforts to restore our rights, we must know who is truly with us." He turned and faced Morgan. "And who is not."

"I am *with* what is right," said Morgan strongly. Every man looked at Morgan and waited for his next reply. "And what is right is that we decide our own destiny without foolish, hasty decisions," he stated.

"And just what does that mean?" asked Isaac Hartley.

"We must still act in good faith, even though the Crown has closed the harbor and suspended our legislative rights," explained Morgan. "Haste has its price, especially when fueled by too much rum and ale."

"Indeed," remarked Wilcox.

"Then what do you propose, Will?" asked Rodgers.

"We should make one more plea — one more peaceful plea — for justice, for fairness," said Morgan.

"Enough of peaceful pleas," remarked Bateman.

"No," continued Morgan. "We have an obligation to reconcile our differences despite the blood that has been shed."

"And if the Crown refuses?" asked Rodgers.

Morgan paused and spoke deliberately: "Then, and only then, if that plea is rejected, I will take up arms and fight." Morgan paused again because what he was about to say would be something radically different from any of the conversations.

"But I will not fight for a return of the rule of Parliament and George the Third," stated Morgan. "It will be a fight for freedom, a fight for self-governance."

"Self-governance?" said Rodgers.

"Yes, my good-natured friend," said Morgan. "And not just in Massachusetts — all of the colonies."

"That is hardly what I have suggested," said Wilcox. Hadley smirked at Wilcox's displeasure. "A restoration of our rights as Englishmen is appropriate enough, I assure you. Morgan first proposes reconciliation with the Crown and now he advocates the creation of a new form of government."

"We must control our destiny," said Morgan emphatically. "All of the colonies together — and together as one."

"You sound like Samuel Adams," replied Wilcox.

"And what's wrong with that?" questioned Bateman, who was impressed by Morgan's comments.

"But we have a Continental Congress," said John Errol, the eye patch-wearing merchant. "A new government body, to be sure, but a congress nonetheless."

"The Congress?" said Morgan sarcastically. "That group is like a boat without a rudder. And it still acknowledges the King as the sovereign over us all."

"Who then should have the power?" asked Errol.

"The people," said Morgan.

"Aye!" exclaimed Bateman.

"It will take a powerful argument to convince General Gage of that," chuckled Rodgers.

"And how would you convince him of that, especially after all of this bloodshed?" asked Bateman.

"With an expression of civility," explained Wilcox. "A direct appeal to General Gage — to his good sense."

Hadley poured the remains of his tankard over Wilcox's head. Wilcox lunged at Hadley and they both fell to the floor.

"Here they go again," said Rodgers, who realized that the thoughtful debate had been replaced by the developing fisticuffs.

The fight sounded like a full-scale battle as the two grunted and groaned. But it was hardly a memorable struggle; as a matter of fact, the two men rolled around the floor more than they struck each other with their fists. Still, the men cheered them on. It was more like harmless entertainment than genuine aggression.

Wilcox's coat got hooked on a raised floor nail that made a tear along the length of his left sleeve. Wilcox stopped fighting for a moment and examined his torn coat; he became angrier. He threw Hadley against a wooden bench and jumped on him. The pair tumbled together towards the fireplace. The Hartwell brothers quickly lifted a lantern off of a nearby table before Wilcox and Hadley rolled into it.

After a few minutes of inconclusive roughhouse action, the men separated them as they had done on previous occasions that had also been fueled by ale and rum. Morgan held Wilcox firmly as Rodgers assisted Hadley to his feet. Hadley swung widely at Wilcox, but missed and broke a shelf lined with pewter mugs.

The sound of the pewter mugs brought the elder Hartwell from his kitchen. The tavern owner stood in the doorway with his hands on his hips, a signal that the fighting would end immediately.

"That's all for tonight, lads," said Rodgers, grinning as he guided Hadley to the entrance. Hadley reached into his haversack and handed Hartwell a coin. It was Hadley's way of apologizing for the damage to the shelf. Morgan dusted off Wilcox's coat before he escorted him to the back door.

"So much for civilized discussion," said Morgan with a shrug. The rest of the men soon left the tavern for their homes. Bateman tipped his hat to Morgan and smiled. Morgan and Rodgers quickly finished their drinks and grabbed their coats. They stood outside the doorway and watched their friends disappear around the corner of the nearby blacksmith shop.

"Our conversation seemed to be getting somewhere until Hadley and Wilcox went at it again," lamented Rodgers as he draped his linen hunting frock over his shoulders. "Your idea about self-government caught us off guard, Will. Most interesting, to be sure. But what do you think will happen next? A negotiated truce? Another fight?"

Morgan seemed to appear deep in thought. Rodgers anticipated a profound reply from his friend.

"The chickens," said Morgan.

"Chickens?" questioned Rodgers.

"Indeed, Joseph," replied Morgan with a subtle smile. "Chickens."

"What about chickens?" replied Rodgers, who looked dumbfounded.

"The chickens will be fed first in the morning," explained Morgan. "I have a farm to run and a family to care for. As I said, those responsibilities occupy me enough. Good night, Joseph."

Rodgers was flabbergasted by Morgan's reply.

"Are you serious, William Morgan?" lamented Rodgers as his friend walked away into the darkness. "What of your talk of self-government? The people?"

Morgan turned the corner and was gone. Rodgers adjusted his tricorn hat, shook his head, and spoke to himself: "Chickens!" And then he smiled.

PART TWO

The Morgan Farm

"I cannot lie to my children."

William Morgan looked over his farm. The sun had barely risen, but all of the Morgans were already busy with their morning chores. Morgan's wife, Rachel, was preparing breakfast. His daughter, Elizabeth, a red-headed ten-year-old, was collecting eggs from the hen house while his thirteen-year-old son, Jeremiah, fed the animals. Morgan was replacing rails on the fence that bordered the sheep pasture.

Inside the hen house, Elizabeth carefully placed several eggs in her basket. Of all the tasks she had to accomplish during the day, this was her favorite. She had cared for all the hens since they hatched and she had given each of them a name. After she filled the basket, she shuffled through the straw to the door.

"Thanks, Minerva," said Elizabeth to her favorite hen. "See you tomorrow."

As Elizabeth exited, she saw her brother playing soldier near the barn. He was making believe he was firing a musket. It was only a long stick, but Jeremiah imagined it to be an actual flintlock weapon. He had studied his father during militia drills and had memorized the steps needed to load and fire a musket.

Jeremiah confidently tore open the imaginary paper cartridge with his teeth and poured some of the gunpowder inside the small priming pan of the elm-branch flintlock. He closed the pan and poured the rest of the cartridge in the muzzle of his weapon. Then he removed the ramrod and rammed the charge down the muzzle until it rested at the breech. He returned the ramrod, cocked his makeshift musket, aimed, and fired.

"Kapow!" said Jeremiah convincingly. He placed the stick at his side and stood at attention.

Elizabeth had seen him do this before, but never before breakfast.

Morgan lifted one of the rails in place and smiled as he watched his son. He knew Jeremiah was drilling as if he were in the militia; as a matter of fact, the sound of his son's invisible musket had been a familiar one since April 19.

Jeremiah loaded his make-believe flintlock again as his father approached from the other side of the barn.

"Kapow!"

"Excuse me, general, isn't it time to feed the chickens?" asked Elizabeth. Morgan smiled again.

"You sure spoil things good," complained Jeremiah, who could not understand why his sister interrupted such important martial behavior.

"Elizabeth is right, Jeremiah," said Morgan. "Do your chores now, son."

"But, Father, I've got to be ready," said Jeremiah. Morgan looked sternly at his son and took the stick from his hands. Morgan renewed his smile as Jeremiah headed toward the hen house. When Jeremiah passed Elizabeth, he stuck his tongue out at her. She replied in the same way, as if it were a familiar family ritual.

Rachel walked out of the house, wiped her flour-covered hands on her apron, and approached her husband and daughter.

"Father, will there be more fighting?" asked Elizabeth.

"I don't know, child," said Morgan. "Time will tell."

"Take the eggs to the table," ordered Rachel. "Go on. And no running!"

After Elizabeth entered the house, Rachel stared at her husband. He smiled at her, but she did not return the expression.

"Time will tell?" asked Rachel. "Is that the kind of answer that brings comfort to your daughter and to me?"

Before Morgan could reply, Rachel continued with her lecture.

"And you allow your son to sport as a member of the militia when he is too young to even consider such a status — as if I would allow such a thing if he were of age," lectured Rachel.

"I cannot lie to my children," said Morgan. "You know that, my dear."

Rachel rubbed her hands across her face and regained her composure.

"So much has changed since the Tea Party, William," said Rachel. "It was joyous then, in a way: the cheers and good spirits. But now, the Crown has closed the harbor, suspended our charter, our assembly."

"These are difficult times, to be sure," said Morgan. "But there will be a resolution to all of this."

"Only if Parliament and the King deem it so," replied Rachel. "They are the authority."

"The right to govern us, to tax us, should be done by us, not them," intoned Morgan solemnly.

"Then tell that to the King's soldiers," replied Rachel sarcastically. "They're waiting for you in Boston."

"I intend to," stated Morgan.

Rachel was stunned by his reply. "Like Samuel Hadley, who was killed with the others on Lexington Green?"

"If people are to be free, truly free, then a high price must be paid for that freedom," said Morgan. He turned and walked towards the house.

"Not at the cost of our family," whispered Rachel to herself.

PART THREE

A Father and Son

"I remember everything about Mama."

Joshua Hudson's farm was located only a mile away from Morgan's, but it was so very different. It was more like a large garden; in fact, it was less than half the size of Morgan's sheep pasture. And it seemed to have more than its share of rocks imbedded in the soil. But it was Hudson's property. Not every black man in Lincoln, Massachusetts, owned land; in fact, most were not even free. Slavery existed in all thirteen British colonies; Massachusetts had used slave labor since the 1630s and the colony was the center of the New England slave trade.

Hudson and his family had been slaves in New Jersey. They had been the property of a doctor who practiced in New Brunswick. But in the early winter of 1756, Hudson and his family fled to Massachusetts, where he worked as a laborer for an abolitionist who gave him lodging. Hudson was given a small wage for his labor and it took him almost seven years to save enough money to buy three acres of land.

Hudson's wife had died nearly three years ago of smallpox. She had managed to raise her only child, Luke, now nearly fourteen years old, as well as any mother in Massachusetts. She taught Luke how to read, be truthful, be helpful to his father, and respectful of the Sabbath. Hudson appreciated that she taught Luke well.

Hudson and Luke were busy working on their land. Hudson stuck his shovel into the ground and it clanked as it struck another field stone. He leaned over and pulled a large jagged rock from his rye field and placed it in the two-wheeled cart.

"That's a full load, son," said Hudson, as he wiped the sweat from his face with the edge of his shirt sleeve. "Take 'em away."

Luke positioned himself between the cart's two carrying poles and lifted. He pulled the cart across the field towards an irregular rock wall. The cart's wheels followed the furrows that had been made by three previous cart loads of fieldstone. Luke removed each rock and placed it in position next to the others on the jagged wall, a task he had done many times before. The rock wall was nearly three feet tall and almost one hundred feet long. It extended from Hudson's simple frame house to his cattle pen, where two fine dairy cows roamed.

Hudson was used to removing rocks from fields. He did the same task when he was a boy toiling for his former master. Although it was still hard work — in fact, it was clearly more difficult for him now at age thirty-five than it was when he was fifteen — there was a sense of pride in his labor because Hudson knew that it was *his* land. He belonged to no man other than himself. He had made a personal promise that he would work hard enough to make his land as successful as any in the area because one day, the land would be Luke's.

"It's lookin' fine," shouted Hudson. "Fine, indeed."

Luke smiled. He appreciated his father's compliment.

Hudson removed a few more rocks as Luke returned with the cart.

"Time for breakfast?" noted Hudson as he rinsed his hands with water from a gallon-sized barrel.

"I can work a bit longer, Father," replied Luke.

"Can you, now?" asked Hudson, who admired his son's willingness to work hard.

"I can pull another cartload, at least," said Luke proudly.

"But I can't," said Hudson with a grin. "Let's eat."

Luke washed his hands and followed his father to a tree, where a linen sack hung from a branch. Hudson removed the sack, sat down, and opened it. He removed a few pieces of dried beef and several biscuits. He handed Luke a biscuit, who attempted to take a quick bite.

"Wait now, Luke," instructed Hudson. "Let's not forget to give thanks for what we got."

"Yes, sir," replied Luke, who then bowed his head.

"Almighty God, we thank you for your generosity of these gifts which we are about to partake," said Hudson solemnly. "May we be truly grateful. Amen."

"Amen!" stated Luke, who promptly bit into the biscuit.

"I thought you said you could work a bit longer?" asked Hudson. "It looks like the biscuit changed your mind."

"Seems like," replied Luke with a sheepish grin. "You know, these are tastin' almost as good as those Mama used to make."

"Just *almost*?" said Hudson.

"Almost," replied Luke with a warm smile.

"You remember those biscuits?" asked Hudson.

"I remember everything about Mama," said Luke.
"So do I, son," said Hudson. "So do I."

PART FOUR

General Israel Putnam

"And for that, I need your help."

Israel Putnam had accomplished more in his fifty-seven years than any of the other militia officers who sat around the large wooden table inside the dining room of loyalist Isaac Royall's house, a fine home that had been confiscated by the Massachusetts General Court. Putnam had served in Major Robert Rogers' Rangers during the French and Indian War and had risen to the rank of major. On August 8, 1758, Putnam was captured by Mohawk warriors near Crown Point, New York, and tied to a post, where he was going to be burned alive. However, a French officer interceded on his behalf and saved his life. A year later, Putnam led his regiment in the successful capture of Fort Carillon, which was renamed Fort Ticonderoga. In 1760, Putnam was part of the large British offensive which forced the French to surrender Montreal. And Putnam commanded troops during Pontiac's Rebellion in 1763.

"Gentlemen!" stated Putnam boldly. "As you know, the Massachusetts Provincial Congress has learned that the King's troops are preparing to secure and hold the Dorchester and Charlestown Necks. And now the Committee of Safety is requiring that defenses be built to protect these vital areas from attack. General Ward has ordered me to construct the defenses on the Charlestown Neck. And for that, I need your help."

"What kind of defenses?" asked Colonel William Prescott of the Pepperell Militia.

"Dirt, rocks, stones, fence posts," replied Putnam. "Anything we can throw up quickly."

"So what you are asking us to do is…" said Prescott.

"I am asking you to command, colonel!" interrupted Putnam. "How you get the men to build it will be based upon your leadership and your resourcefulness."

Putnam stared at Prescott and then looked every other officer in the eyes. "Do you understand, gentlemen?"

Every man nodded yes.

"Of course, we do not have the time to construct something worthy of true field fortifications, but I know each of you will rise to the occasion," said Putnam. "Are there any additional questions regarding our task? Are there any other questions?"

"Yes, general," replied Colonel John Stark. "Where are we going to get powder from? We are running very low. Most of my men don't even have full cartridge boxes."

"Same with my men, sir," added Prescott.

"We will have to do with what we have," replied Putnam.

"With all due respect, sir, how will we accomplish that?" asked Prescott with a sense of urgency.

Putnam paused. He was well aware of the militias' shortage of gunpowder, but he had already devised a plan — albeit a risky one — to maximize their limited firepower. "You will instruct your men to withhold their volleys until they can see the whites of the eyes of the regulars upon their advance," stated Putnam. "And then when they get that close, and only then, will you command them to fire. That is the only way we can make the most of what we have."

Putnam rose from his chair and the other officers stood.

"Gentlemen, may Providence be with us," said Putnam.

PART FIVE

The Ride of Joseph Rodgers

"All the men are going."

The Morgans sat at the breakfast table and finished the last pieces of bread that Rachel had baked earlier that morning.

"Father?" asked Jeremiah as he wiped his mouth and placed his napkin on the table, "does the musket lock face forward in the command 'rest-your-firelocks?'"

Morgan was about to answer his son's question, but Rachel's stare altered his reply. He had seen that expression before. He looked at his son. "There's a stable to rake and I want it done now," demanded Morgan. "Off with you. You, too, Elizabeth."

The children promptly left the house.

Rachel maintained her stare.

"He was just asking a simple question," reasoned Morgan.

"A question about muskets followed, no doubt, by one about the militia and then one about fighting and killing, to be sure," said Rachel.

"All the boys his age act as if they were in the militia," noted Morgan.

"What other boys?" asked Rachel. "Name one."

"Luke Hudson, for one," stated Morgan.

"Joshua Hudson has more than enough to do on that poor excuse of a farm than to allow his son to engage in such foolish idleness," said Rachel firmly. She had made her point and began clearing the table.

"Speaking of idleness, I'll get back to the fence now," he said with a cautious smile.

Rachel's serious expression soon melted into a slight smile.

"I could use more firewood," said Rachel. "Water doesn't boil on its own, at least not in this house."

"Your obedient servant, your Majesty!" replied Morgan, bowing at his wife. Rachel's smile widened as Morgan hastened out the door.

The rail fence that encircled the sheep pasture always needed repair in June. The spring rains loosed the soil around some of the posts, which made them vulnerable to both the actions of sheep and children. Fortunately, there were fewer posts to reset this year despite the wet weather in April and May.

After a few hours of work, Morgan was nearly finished. He lifted the last rail in place. Rachel walked to him with a cup of water. As he drank, he turned and looked at Jeremiah and Elizabeth, who were sitting under a large oak tree sharing a dried apple and a piece of corn bread. Morgan sensed the harmony and tranquility of his life with his family. He drew a deep breath and appeared content. Rachel understood the look on her husband's face and quickly recited a quiet prayer of gratitude. He noticed what she was doing. When Rachel lifted her head, Morgan replied, "Amen, my dear."

"May it always be like this," remarked Rachel as she held her husband's hands. Morgan placed his arms around Rachel and held her closely. But the peacefulness of the moment was interrupted by the sound of cantering hooves. A horseback rider approached from the east.

"That looks like Joseph Rodgers," said Rachel. "What would he be doing here?"

The Morgans walked back to the barn, where they were greeted by Rodgers.

"Mrs. Morgan," greeted Rodgers politely. But Rachel sensed that something was wrong.

"Will, turn out!" instructed Rodgers. "We're forming on the road to Charlestown Neck."

Rachel held her children's hands, but she grasped Jeremiah's hand more tightly.

"And bring a shovel," said Rodgers.

"A shovel?" questioned Morgan.

"As well as your firelock," added Rodgers. "We have learned that General Gage plans to take the heights outside of Boston."

"I had hoped for reconciliation," remarked Morgan.

"We're beyond that now," stated Rodgers. "Gage has seen to that. And Parliament. And King George."

Jeremiah broke away from his mother. "May I come along, Father?" asked Jeremiah enthusiastically. "I can help!"

"We could use as many to dig as possible," said Rodgers.

Morgan exchanged looks with Rachel, who was becoming more frightened by the minute. He turned to his son — and for a moment, he remembered Jeremiah's birth and the rapid passage of over a dozen years.

"I don't think so," said Morgan.

"But Father!" pleaded Jeremiah.

"Tell Sergeant Smith that I will be along shortly," said Morgan. Rodgers turned his horse and rode off. Morgan could see the disappointment on his son's face and the expression of relief in Rachel's guarded smile.

"Must you go?" pleaded Rachel as she gently touched her husband's arm.

"All the men are going," said Morgan.

"Then I will go, too," remarked Jeremiah proudly. Rachel looked displeased, but her daughter unintentionally lightened the moment with a question.

"If Jeremiah leaves, will I have to do his chores, too?" asked Elizabeth. Morgan tried to restrain his smile. Rachel momentarily relaxed.

"Please," said Jeremiah to to his mother.

"Your father said 'no!'" scolded Rachel.

"He said he 'didn't think so,' Mother," clarified Jeremiah. He turned to his father and displayed a look of desperation. Morgan's protective posture started to weaken. He knew how much Jeremiah wanted to be part of anything that the militia did.

"Look, Rachel, all he will do is dig," explained Morgan. "Dig *what*, I do not know. But he will not be shouldering a musket. I promise you that. And then I will send him home."

Rachel said nothing. She awaited a more convincing explanation.

"He is not a child anymore, my dear," said Morgan. Jeremiah beamed as his father spoke. "And, yes, I know that he is not yet a man." Elizabeth stuck her tongue out at Jeremiah, but this time, he did not return the gesture because he now considered it to be child's play. "But there will be important times in his life that will lead up to that day," explained Morgan. "This may be one of them — an opportunity for your son to grow up, to accept responsibility. And with his father at his side."

Rachel was still unconvinced.

"Please, Mother," said Jeremiah.

For a moment, they all silently stood in place. It felt like an eternity to Morgan and Jeremiah.

Rachel took a deep breath and exhaled. "How long will you two be gone?" she asked. Jeremiah stood erect and thrust his chest out.

"It will probably be sunset by the time we get to the Neck, so I assume we'll work into the night," said Morgan. "I'll send him home in the morning."

"And you?" asked Rachel.

"When all of the men return, I will return," stated Morgan emphatically. "Fear not, my love."

PART SIX

The March to Charlestown Neck

"Make peace with your Creator now."

Morgan and Jeremiah walked over the crest at the south end of the sheep pasture and saw the road. It was already filled with men carrying muskets and shovels; a few pulled two-wheel wooden carts. They quickly joined the growing ranks of fellow farmers, shopkeepers, and tradesmen who were led by Sergeant Matthew Smith, a rugged French and Indian War veteran and former schoolmaster. A few boys were among the men, but Jeremiah did not know any of them.

After an hour of walking, Sergeant Smith called a halt.

"All right, then, rest a moment," ordered Smith. "We'll be marching again soon enough."

Jeremiah saw Joshua Hudson and Luke emerge from the tree line with a group of other armed men, including Thomas Hadley. "Luke!" shouted Jeremiah.

"Jeremiah!" replied Luke. The two boys ran up to each other and shared a mutual grin.

Joshua Hudson acknowledged Morgan. "You couldn't say 'no' either, eh, Joshua?" said Morgan.

"It seems that I said it as well as you did," laughed Hudson.

"'Tis good to see you again," remarked Morgan.

Jeremiah and Luke shouldered their shovels as if they were muskets and stood behind their fathers.

"How are Rachel and Elizabeth?" asked Hudson.

"Fine, thank you, though Rachel is worried about Jeremiah being here," said Morgan.

"That's understandable," replied Hudson. "I'm still questioning myself about allowing Luke to be with me."

"What have you heard about all this?" asked Morgan.

"Captain Josephson said they needed folks with tools for building,'" said Hudson.

"Build, not dig?" questioned Morgan. "But build just what?"

"A fort," stated Hudson. "That's what I heard." Luke and Jeremiah were pleasantly surprised by the news.

"Once again, I'm the last to know," said Morgan with a smile.

"Such is the fate of all militia privates," laughed Hudson.

"A fort is it, but where?" asked Morgan of Sergeant Smith.

"Aye, lads," said Smith. "We're going up to Bunker Hill to build us a redoubt."

"Bunker Hill?" asked Morgan. "That's by Charlestown. For what reason?"

"General Putnam told Colonel Prescott, who told Captain Josephson, who told me, and I'm tellin' you: we're inviting the King's soldiers out of Boston to give 'em a taste of our powder and shot," explained Smith. Jeremiah and Luke were gleeful over the news.

"If General Gage sees such fortifications, he will know that we can place artillery there," said Morgan.

"And with those guns in position, his entire force — and much of Boston — could be destroyed," added Hudson.

"So he has to attack first," reasoned Morgan. "And he could do that easily enough while the redoubt was being built. His guns would destroy us before we could get our shovels in the ground."

"Not if it's built without him seeing it," said Smith.

"What?" asked Morgan.

"Impossible," stated Hudson firmly.

Morgan thought carefully about Sergeant Smith's reasoning. "The only way that could happen is if everything was built in the darkness of a single night," reasoned Morgan.

Sergeant Smith rubbed his nose as he acknowledged Morgan's reply. Then Smith smiled. "Now keep this all under your hats, lads," said Smith, looking around. "It's not for everyone to know right now. We've known each other for quite some time and I know I can trust you both. But, in due time, everyone in the ranks will know." Morgan and Hudson understood Smith's request. They looked at Jeremiah and Luke. Both boys acknowledged their fathers with a nod of understanding.

"All right then, form up!" shouted Sergeant Smith to his group. "That be enough rest for any man!"

Jeremiah walked up to Smith and saluted with his shovel. Smith returned his salute with a guarded smile

"What exactly is a redoubt, sergeant?" asked Jeremiah.

As a non-commissioned officer in a militia company, Smith did not have to answer every military question posed to him, particularly from a boy who was not even old enough to shoulder a firelock. But Smith was a former teacher and he relished the opportunity to instruct and inform at every opportunity.

"An enclosed defensive emplacement, me boy," said Smith as if he were still standing in front of the old Cambridge schoolhouse.

But the sergeant's explanation didn't make much sense to Jeremiah, who squinted and shook his head. Like any effective teacher, Smith simplified his answer.

"Think of a large roofless house with piles of dirt and stone for walls," said Smith.

Jeremiah understood.

"Thank you, sergeant," said Jeremiah as he turned and walked away.

"Stop right there, soldier!" ordered Smith. Jeremiah stopped instantly and turned back to Smith.

"You forgot to salute, private," said Smith.

Jeremiah saluted and smiled. Smith returned the salute.

Within minutes, the colonists were on the march again. At every turn in the road, more men with shovels and muskets joined the growing ranks. Timothy Goode, a baker, reported with only his shovel. As a Quaker, he did not own a musket and pledged never to take the life of another man. But he wanted to show his contempt for Parliament's Intolerable Acts, which, he believed, were a threat to the liberties of all the colonists.

"There's Richard Bell," said Hudson, pointing to a small group of men approaching from the south.

"Ah, there's that straw hat of his," noted Morgan. "You could identify him with that a mile away." Bell, a cooper by trade, was a minuteman who had participated in the fight at Concord. Hudson and Morgan raised their muskets at Bell, who returned the greeting.

Thomas Hadley approached Morgan.

"Well, Morgan, I thought you wanted to wait for reconciliation?" asked Hadley.

"It appears the situation has changed," replied Morgan. "You remember what I said at Hartwell's."

"Indeed," remarked Hadley. "Oh, I'm sorry about my words last night. They came from the bottom of a mug of ale."

"Perhaps more than just a single mug, Thomas," noted Morgan.

"Indeed," said Hadley with a sheepish grin.

"Tomorrow night, we'll all have a drink together once again," suggested Goode.

"Aye," replied Hadley.

"Tomorrow night is a long time away, lads," said Morgan.

The men and boys continued their march. Another hour passed before the group stopped again. Nearby, a tall minister emerged from the doorway of an inn. The officers beckoned their men to stand around the clergyman.

"He looks familiar," whispered Morgan to Hudson.

"Very," replied Hudson. "It's Reverend Bakewell. He prayed over my wife before she died."

Bakewell took a step forward and removed his black tricorn hat. All the men removed their hats in turn and bowed their heads.

"Make peace with your Creator now," instructed Bakewell. "Speak to Him in prayer, for ye may speak to Him in His Kingdom on the morrow."

For several minutes, all the men participated in silent prayers. Some took only a few moments; others took minutes to complete. While Morgan bowed his head, he thought he heard a man sob. Bakewell looked up and waited for every man to finish his prayer. When the last man raised his head, the minister stepped back and lifted both of his arms into the air.

"May Providence favor our undertakings in the days ahead," concluded Bakewell. "Amen."

"Amen" echoed through the ranks.

As the men reformed their companies, Hudson noticed that Joseph Rodgers was slightly limping.

"What's the matter?" asked Hudson.

"My feet," uttered Joseph Rodgers. "They hurt like the blazes. I wish I could have ridden my horse to wherever we're going. I miss him."

"I'm sure he feels the same way about you, Joseph," said Morgan as the men nearby laughed.

By the time the colonists reached the Charlestown Neck, it was dusk. Thousands of colonists had gathered there. Local militia units merged with armed colonial groups from Connecticut and New Hampshire.

"I've never seen so many militia men in all my life," exclaimed Luke.

"And I've never walked so far in my life," said Jeremiah to Luke.

"Me, too," said Luke. "My shovel weighed a lot less when we started."

"It appears that a few of our volunteers are getting tired," remarked Hudson with a subtle grin.

"Not me!" replied Luke.

"Nor I," said Jeremiah.

"I hope not," said Morgan. "For the night is young and we have yet to work. But when that work is done, you will return home."

Captain Edward Josephson walked up to Sergeant Smith, who promptly saluted. Josephson, thirty-six years old, was a prosperous lawyer who had fought in the Battle of Fort Niagara during the French and Indian War. Well respected by the men, Josephson had been elected to command the company last autumn.

"Now then, sergeant, when it's completely dark, lead your men there," instructed Josephson as he pointed to a place near one of the nearby hills further down the Charlestown Neck. "We will start building our fortifications when Gridley's men join us."

Everyone sat on the ground and waited. Jeremiah and Luke shared a drink of water from a canteen. Joseph Rodgers removed his shoes and rubbed his sore feet. "Ah, that feels a bit better," he remarked.

An hour passed.

Another militia company arrived and joined them. Captain Josephson engaged in a brief discussion with the other officer while the new arrivals rested on the ground. One man placed his shovel and musket on a large rock. "We've just been told we're building a redoubt, whatever that is," he explained to a companion.

"An enclosed defensive emplacement," stated Jeremiah.

Sergeant Smith smiled.

Captain Josephson nodded to Smith, who stood up and gestured to the men to follow. "No magpie chatter now, lads," stated Smith. "We don't want to wake up General Gage just yet."

Josephson's company quietly walked in a single file past Bunker Hill. They continued to the next hill on the Charlestown Peninsula.

"I wonder what they call this?" questioned Hudson.

"Breed's Hill," said Smith.

PART SEVEN

Building the Defenses

"The hands of Providence can be so generous."

An hour later, two additional companies arrived at the place where digging had commenced. Hundreds of shovels were pressed into the soil. The dirt and stones were carefully piled along designated lines marked by the militia sergeants from each company.

"I just heard that we're building a redoubt," said one of the militiamen in Gridley's company to Morgan.

"We've known that since this afternoon," said Morgan quietly.

"I heard it was secret information," questioned the militiaman.

"So much for secrets," whispered Hudson.

"And I heard there's hardly a bayonet to be had among us," said the militiaman.

Jeremiah's shovel hit Luke's and made a noticeable clank. "Careful now," scolded William Morgan. "We can't make any unnecessary noise."

"Sorry, Father," apologized Jeremiah as he leaned on his shovel.

"Back to work, son," urged Morgan.

Jeremiah took a step to the right of Luke and continued to dig. The shoveling went on for hours. It was well past midnight when the fortifications took shape.

"It's starting to look like something," said Bell as he removed his straw hat and wiped his forehead with his shirt sleeve.

"But look like what?' questioned Goode. "This wall of dirt barely reaches my knees."

"Keep digging, lads," said Sergeant Smith. "It will be higher than your heads by dawn."

Smith climbed to the top of the redoubt and looked at its outside base. He noticed that in certain spots, excess piles of dirt and rocks lessened the distance between the top of the wall and the ground. Smith thought that these small mounds would make it easy for an attacking foot soldier to scale the wall. "Now then, Morgan, Hudson, your boys, and Joseph

Rodgers: move to the outside here and shovel these piles back on the walls," he commanded. "And move some of these larger stones away from the wall."

The group climbed over the wall and started to shovel. Morgan paused at the top and looked towards Boston. Candlelight could be seen in the windows of a few buildings near the wharf. Lanterns shone brightly from all of the Royal Navy ships, especially the HMS *Lively*, which was anchored in the Charles River.

Everything looked so peaceful. Morgan was fond of Boston. He had met and courted Rachel there. He remembered how Elizabeth and Jeremiah had enjoyed visiting their grandparents, who lived not far from the wharf where the Boston Tea Party had taken place. Rachel was correct, he thought: it had been joyous then. But that seemed so long ago.

Morgan figured that the first light of dawn would be visible in less than an hour. Hudson smirked as he placed another shovelful of dirt on the growing wall.

"What amuses you so?" asked Morgan as he walked off the wall.

"Of all the tasks we should be assigned, we get to dig," said Hudson.

"And?" questioned Morgan.

"Let's just say I have experience in that area," noted Hudson.

"Enough of that chatter, lads," said Sergeant Smith. "Those Redcoat sentries have ears as keen as hounds."

Hudson and Morgan exchanged smiles and resumed digging. Luke and Jeremiah saw their fathers smile and broke into grins of their own.

"We're here," whispered Jeremiah. "Here in the militia." Luke smiled in agreement.

Jeremiah's shovel lightly touched a large rock. He placed his shovel under the rock and pushed down on the handle, but the stone barely moved. Luke pushed the rock as Jeremiah tried to force it loose with his shovel. They worked well together and it started to move. After they freed the stone from the soil, they confronted another one.

Sergeant Smith walked towards the boys and encouraged them on. "Good," said Smith. "Now get your backs into it, men!" Jeremiah and Luke paused for a moment in joyous disbelief. They had heard the sergeant address them before as "lads" and "boys," but never as "men." Smith's words were encouraging. The stone weighed more than both of them, but they rolled it nearly ten feet away from the redoubt's outside wall.

"This is harder than I thought," said Luke.

"It's better than feeding chickens," explained Jeremiah.

"But we're in the militia now," noted Luke as he looked at his father.

"You're not in the militia," corrected Hudson. "You're working *alongside* the militia."

"I told your mother, Jeremiah, that as soon as this gets built, you're going home," said Morgan.

"And that goes for you, too, Luke," added Hudson. "But until then, we have work to do."

Sergeant Smith approached them. "I thought we were going to build this back at Bunker Hill?" said Morgan.

"We were, but Breed's Hill here is even closer to General Gage," explained Smith.

"General Gage is not gonna like this when he sees it," laughed Hudson.

"And that's what we're counting on," replied Smith as he rubbed his nose. "All right, lads, back to work."

The humidity still lingered in the predawn darkness. Morgan placed his hat and coat on a nearby stack of muskets. Jeremiah did the same. They both walked back to their section of the wall and resumed shoveling. An hour passed before the men saw Sergeant Smith again. Everyone was nearly exhausted.

"Take your rest," commanded Smith as he placed a small keg of water on the ground. "Mind yourselves, lads. Not enough for a full drink." Smith carefully poured a few ounces of water in a small tin cup and passed it around. He rationed the rest of the water until the keg was empty. Morgan didn't drink because he had a few mouthfuls of water left in his canteen. He planned to share the water with his son when they had finished their work.

Smith looked towards the east. "It will be light soon," he said.

Jeremiah and Luke sat down where they stood. The sounds of shovels had been replaced by the sounds of crickets.

"You tired?" asked Jeremiah.

"I'm more hungry than tired," said Luke.

Joshua Hudson handed his son a biscuit. Luke broke off a piece and gave it to Jeremiah. Both boys ate the biscuits as if they hadn't eaten in days.

Hudson sat down next to his son and finished eating.

Captain Josephson walked past Morgan and Hudson to where several stacks of muskets stood. He counted the muskets and moved on.

Luke looked at his father. "Are they gonna make you a captain someday?" asked Luke.

"Captain Joshua Hudson, eh?" said Hudson. "No, I don't think so. I reckon I'll stay a private like most of the men."

"Was grandpa a private, too?" asked Luke

"No, grandpa wasn't allowed," explained Hudson, recalling the life of slavery that his father endured. "He wasn't free." Hudson's eyes misted up as he remembered his father.

"I'm glad we're free," stated Luke.

"Free we are," said Hudson.

"Then as a free man, I'm gonna join the militia, too," noted Luke proudly.

"We'll talk about the militia when you're sixteen," said Hudson with a guarded smile. "Now finish your biscuit."

Some of the men quickly fell asleep. Some sat back and ate food from their haversacks. Some prayed.

Several militiamen from Medford arrived with a cart full of tree limbs and wooden planks. They unloaded some of the planks and placed them at the inner base of one of the walls. The planks would serve as level steps where the men could more comfortably fire at any attacking force. After the wood was placed in position, the men rested. But soon a discussion developed among the men.

"When the sun comes up, all hell will break loose around here," said Bradley Quinn, a farmer from Medford. Several men nodded in agreement. "But I still believe we can resolve our differences with England."

Thomas Hadley couldn't believe his ears that another man favored reconciliation with the Crown, especially at this particular juncture.

"You must be a friend of Ebeneezer Wilcox, eh?" asked Hadley with a bit of sarcasm.

"Never heard of him," replied Quinn.

"Well, it be a tad bit late for resolution now," said Thomas Russell, another man from Medford.

"It is never too late," reasoned Quinn. "We can stop a potential battle before it starts."

"And how do you propose to do that?" said Russell.

"With a petition," replied Quinn.

"A petition?" questioned Russell.

"Exactly, Russel!" said Quinn.

Russell shook his head in disbelief and scowled.

"Well, why don't you go down right now and petition General Gage in person," said Russell dramatically. "My dear general: Me and me neighbors, who right now are building a secret fortification right under your nose, kindly request that all of our rights be restored. Thank you kindly, your most obedient servant."

The men chuckled, but Quinn did not crack a smile.

"When General Gage sees what we've built, you'll meet him soon enough," explained Morgan.

"Him and about a thousand regulars," added Hudson.

"A thousand?" asked Goode. "You think that many?"

"Maybe more," said Russell. Small conversations erupted among the men about the size of General Gage's army.

"I wonder when Congress will send more men here?" asked Quinn.

"Send here?" said Russell. "You think they even formed an army yet? There's nothing to send."

Russell's remarks seemed to strike fear in the eyes of some of the men. "God save us," said another man from Medford. For a moment, there was total silence.

"Then it's up to us to hold this ground," said Jeremiah with grim determination. Jeremiah's words lightened the moment. The men chuckled as Joseph Rodgers tugged on Jeremiah's hat. William Morgan looked at Jeremiah proudly.

Sergeant Smith walked along the redoubt to one of its corners and looked towards Boston. "Well, Tommy Gage, when you see what we've built, you'll be paying us a visit, I'm sure," said Smith to himself. "And when you leave, I'll warrant you won't be forgettin' our hospitality."

Smith walked back to his company. "All right, everybody up," said Smith. "Come on, then. Quiet now. Back to work with you."

"That was quick," said Jeremiah as he stretched his arms outward.

"Too quick," remarked Luke, who examined the blisters on his hands.

The men resumed their shoveling. Another cartful of wooden planks arrived and the Medford men placed them on top of the other boards.

"High enough for you yet?" asked Bell to Goode.

"Not yet," said Goode. "I prefer it a bit higher."

Morgan grabbed one of the planks and placed it against one that Hudson was positioning.

"The sun should be coming up soon," said Morgan.

"Been a long night," said Hudson.

"I think the upcoming day is going to be a whole lot longer," predicted Morgan.

Hudson rested on his shovel. "What do you think is gonna happen?" he asked.

"I'm no general," stated Morgan, "but the first move Gage will probably make today…"

"Not today," interrupted Hudson. "When all of this is over."

"Over?" asked Morgan. "We're just at the beginning. We know how long the war with France lasted. But I am sure of this: There comes a time in your life when you have to make a fateful choice, to do something that's right even though the odds are against you. Today may be one of those times."

"I already had one of those times when I ran away from my master," said Hudson. "Don't need another."

Morgan knew of Hudson's years in slavery. The two friends had discussed it many times at Hartwell's tavern.

"But you're here," said Morgan.

Hudson looked at Luke. "I'm here because of him," explained Hudson. "Because now he can know that his pappy is just as good as any other man."

"And we are just as good as any king who sits on a throne 3,000 miles away," added Morgan.

"Sometimes when I look at Luke sleeping, I feel more blessed than any king," said Hudson. "Do you know what I mean, William?"

"I know what you mean, Joshua," replied Morgan. "I took a drink poured from Rachel's hand yesterday. My children were playing nearby. I was most content. The hands of Providence can be so generous."

"We'll see what Providence has in store for us soon enough, my friend," said Hudson. "Soon enough."

About ten minutes passed before Morgan looked up and saw the first glimpse of the approaching dawn.

The redoubt was near completion. Its longest walls were over 150 feet long. As the sky brightened, the men were able to see its size and shape.

"Ya done good, lads," said Smith. "Tis a fine works, it be."

"Wish this was still a bit higher," said Goode.

"It's better than what they have," said Bell, pointing to the militia who were lined behind a simple rail fence near the water.

Suddenly, a cannon shot fired from the HMS *Lively*. Jeremiah, Luke, and the others who had fallen asleep were quickly awakened. The cannon ball fell short of the redoubt, but several militiamen panicked, dropped their shovels, and ran towards Bunker Hill.

Smith grabbed a man who started to leave his position. "Steady now," smiled Smith. "There's work to be done. Here be your shovel. Take it! You wouldn't want General Gage to have this for his own use now, would you?"

Another cannon blast roared.

A militia man from another company ran up to Sergeant Smith and handed him a written message. Smith read it and quickly shouted: "We need another line of defense! A breastworks. Start here!"

Morgan took Jeremiah's shovel out of his hand. He looked at his son and remembered when Jeremiah was born and when he took his first steps. It seemed like yesterday. He had grown up so quickly. "Go with Luke to Bunker Hill and then get on the road and head home," ordered Morgan.

"But the fighting's here," pleaded Jeremiah.

"Go!" said Morgan.

Jeremiah and Luke looked at each other as the *Lively's* guns fired again. A broadside from another ship followed.

"Get a move on!" shouted Hudson.

Both boys ran towards Bunker Hill.

PART EIGHT

General Gage's Plan

"These farmers will not stand against a disciplined frontal attack."

General Gage had already been awakened by the cannon fire before the orderly knocked on his door.

"I'm awake, sergeant!" shouted the British commander-in-chief from the edge of his bed. "Enter!"

The sergeant entered with two guards. "Sir," he replied.

"What is the meaning of all this commotion?" asked Gage.

"The *Lively* is firing on rebel fortifications across the river," explained the sergeant.

"Fortifications?" asked Gage as he pulled his breeches on. "What fortifications? Where?"

"Near Charlestown, sir," replied the sergeant.

"Since when?" asked Gage.

"Since the overnight, sir," explained the sergeant.

"Get my staff here!" fumed Gage. The soldiers hastily exited.

Gage looked out of his window, but could see nothing. He heard more cannon shots and thought of the *Lively*. It was the ship that had brought him to Boston only a year before when he assumed the position of Royal Governor of Massachusetts. Gage was despised by the people of Boston because he had closed their harbor to trade and suspended their legislature following the Tea Party in 1773.

Within the hour, British generals Henry Clinton, John Burgoyne, and William Howe assembled at a table in Gage's planning room. The three had only arrived in Boston less than a month ago. Gage entered and the others immediately stood.

"Be seated, gentlemen," ordered Gage as he unrolled a map on the table and pointed to several locations. "Besides the previous encampments along this road, reports indicate that they are positioned here in this redoubt and now here behind these field works and along this fence line. If these rebels manage to place artillery on these heights, this entire city is vulnerable."

Gage waited for a reply from his generals.

"Amazing, these provincials," remarked Burgoyne. "They moved as quickly as ants building a mound in a single night."

"And we will crush them like ants," stated Gage emphatically. "As such, we will land here, assault them directly, and control these hills."

"Directly?" questioned Howe.

"Directly!" replied Gage.

General Clinton looked carefully at the map and noticed the narrowness of the Charlestown Neck.

"With all due respect, sir, a landing here at the Neck with but one brigade, perhaps two, will isolate them from their reserves at Cambridge," said Clinton, pointing at the map. "And they will be ours, I assure you." Clinton was convinced that his plan had merit.

Gage shook his head from side to side and then he pointed at another location on the map.

"A commander should never place his army between two enemy armies," argued Gage. "We would be caught in a vise against their greater numbers. No, General Clinton, these farmers will not stand against a disciplined frontal attack from His Majesty's soldiers. We will cross the harbor and General Howe will lead the attack."

"Your servant, sir!" replied Howe.

As the generals left Gage's headquarters, two soldiers on guard duty executed a present arms salute with their muskets and then exchanged glances.

"Looks like we'll be doin' more than standing guard before this day is over," said Geoffrey Thorpe, a private in the 43rd Regiment of Foot.

"I prefer standin' right here, mate," replied Private Errol Vickers with a grin. "Much safer, says I."

Thorpe smiled at the comment.

The two had served together for three years in the regiment before leaving England and arriving in Boston earlier in the year. Thorpe lived in Manchester and Vickers came from Dukinfield, a small town several miles east of the city. As teenagers, they worked in the same textile warehouse, where they met and became friends. Most of the time, the two helped load large textile shipments on wagons. Although the work was physically demanding — the pair labored six twelve-hour days per week — they didn't mind; they were young and hearty. But the work was tedious, repetitive, and uninteresting and they sought to do something else, something more adventurous. So they joined the army. It was actually Thorpe's idea. He had always talked about becoming a soldier, although he knew no one who had served in uniform. Their first years in the regiment were marked by repetitive drilling and martial monotony, activities that undermined Thorpe's early expectations of military excitement. However, the situation changed dramatically when they received orders to ship out to Massachusetts.

Gage's orderly walked up to the soldiers. "Report to your company!" commanded the orderly, who promptly turned and walked away.

"Safer, you said?" asked Thorpe of his friend. "So much for standin' round here, eh?"

By the time Thorpe and Vickers returned to their company barrack, an empty canvas-repair warehouse near the docks, their comrades were busy cleaning their muskets and getting equipped.

"Say, Dexter, what's with that pack?" asked Vickers to a soldier who was completely outfitted for battle. "Marching to Quebec?"

"We're goin' across the river to some hills," said Bradley Dexter, a corporal who hailed from Vickers' hometown. "The rebels built some kind of wall of sorts and General Gage wants it torn down."

"A wooden wall?" asked Thorpe.

"Who knows," remarked Dexter. "Wood or stone, it be comin' down, that's for sure."

"Again, mate, why the pack?" said Vickers. "We'll be over there in a few hours, not a few weeks."

"General Gage's orders," answered Dexter.

"Well then, if I were General Gage…" said Thorpe.

"You're not," interrupted Vickers. "So help me on with me pack, private. And make sure those straps aren't twisted."

PART NINE

The Thunder of British Artillery

"Off you go, boys!"

Copp's Hill was the highest location at the north end of Boston. From the hill, it was easy to see Charlestown across the river and the colonists' fortifications. Royal artillery units that had been positioned on Copp's Hill joined the *Lively* and the other ships and started firing at Breed's Hill. From the colonial field works, the large puffs of white smoke were seen first, then the sound of the guns were heard.

"Get down!" shouted Morgan. Everyone dropped to the ground and pressed against the protective wall of dirt.

Goode slowly peered out over the top of the redoubt.

"Keep your heads down!" shouted Sergeant Smith as his pushed Goode's head below the wall and into the dirt.

"But I can't see anything," countered Goode, who tried to look over the wall.

"I'll look for ya," replied Smith. "Now get down and stay down." A cannon ball skipped along the ground near the redoubt and lodged in the dirt. Goode dropped to the ground and clutched his shovel.

"Up lads, up with ye all," commanded Smith as he climbed atop the breastworks. "Come on, then, put your backs into it."

Another cannonade volley sent Smith sliding into the safe confines of the fortifications. Despite the constant cannon fire, the colonists kept on working.

"Will Morgan!" shouted Smith as another broadside of cannon fire blasted from the *Lively*.

Morgan crawled quickly to Sgt. Smith. "Up here!" commanded Smith. "Quickly now!" They both peered over the breastworks.

"Where are their gun positions?" asked Smith. "Your eyes are better than mine."

Morgan looked carefully at the activity in Boston. "They're firing from the ships and it looks like Copp's Hill," said Morgan, who looked again towards Boston. "Yes, artillery batteries on Copp's Hill."

"Any movement in town?" asked Smith.

"No," noted Morgan. "Nothing, nothing yet. Wait. I see long boats. Barges, too, it seems."

Hudson, Goode, and several other men looked over the dirt wall. They could see small groups of soldiers approaching the boats. Within minutes, hundreds of Redcoats were seen forming at the docks.

"They'll be coming across," said Smith. "That's for sure, lads."

Smith noticed that Goode appeared frightened.

"But it'll take 'em hours before the first boat gets here," reassured Smith. "And it will take 'em even longer to get enough of 'em on this side to mount an attack."

"We've got time then, eh, sergeant?" asked Goode.

"Indeed, lad," replied Smith. "More time to build. Now let's mind our business." The men resumed working amidst cannon blasts from the Royal Navy.

Jeremiah and Luke reached Bunker Hill as another broadside from the *Lively* thundered. They looked back at the redoubt.

"You think those cannons reached?" asked Luke.

"No," stated Jeremiah. "They can't shoot for sour apples."

They walked down the back slope of Bunker Hill and stopped at a cart filled with wooden planks. Jeremiah knew that the planks were needed at the redoubt.

"We should go back," said Jeremiah.

"But our fathers told us something different," replied Luke.

A militiaman confronted them. "Off you go, boys!" he shouted.

"We need this," said another man.

Jeremiah and Luke stepped away from the cart. The two men lifted the arms of the cart and pulled it away.

Suddenly, several men ran past them and headed for the safety of the Cambridge Road. Jeremiah remembered them from yesterday's march. One of the men deliberately dropped his musket before disappearing beyond the tree-lined road.

A minute later, a militia company marched nearby. A militia officer picked the flintlock up and handed it to one of his sergeants, who walked to the rear of the column. As the company marched towards Breed's Hill, Jeremiah noticed a young teenager in the rear rank who carried a musket. "He's our age, Luke!" said Jeremiah as the company marched towards Breed's Hill.

"He's older than us," corrected Luke.

"Only a couple of years," countered Jeremiah. "And I'm almost just about as tall as he is."

"If you're wearin' your hat," noted Luke.

"Look, we both know how to drill and load and fire," said Jeremiah in an effort to convince Luke that they were ready to join the men in battle.

"We load and fire sticks, Jeremiah," remarked Luke. "They're just *sticks*."

PART TEN

Crossing the Charles River

"They're not all rebels."

Dozens of boats filled with the King's troops slowly crossed the Charles River. By the early afternoon, the first boatloads reached the shoreline at Moulton's Point, which was only several hundred yards away from the colonial fieldworks. The Redcoats disembarked near the shoreline and had to walk through the water. The heavy knapsack, which was filled with extra clothing, musket, haversack, canteen, and full cartridge box, made every soldier's advance to dry land more troublesome. Even the drummers and regimental flag bearers had a difficult time trudging their way through the stone-filled, muddy banks.

Once they kicked some of the mud from their footwear, the soldiers quickly formed into company formations under the watchful eyes of their officers. The boatmen promptly rowed back to Boston to get more of General Gage's troops, but due to the strong tides, it took hours to get several thousand Redcoats and artillery pieces across the harbor.

Vickers and Thorpe arrived with the rest of the men in their company at Moulton's Point shortly after two p.m. They disembarked and promptly examined their weapons and accoutrements.

"You'd think that on a beautiful sunny day as this that we'd being doing something else?" said Thorpe to Vickers. "But no, these damned rebels are spoiling me afternoon. And what would I be doing, you might say, if I wasn't here. I should be off duty down at Latham's, having me a tankard of ale as large as a bearskin cap, or perhaps sharing some tea and biscuits with one of the fine ladies of Boston."

Vickers said nothing as he adjusted the strap of his cartridge box.

"There you go," said Thorpe as he straightened out Vickers' strap. "It was twisted."

Vickers stared at Breed's Hill. He could see the field works and the large number of armed colonists. Thorpe realized that his good friend was getting anxious about the upcoming fight, so he tugged on his cartridge box strap. Vickers seemed to emerge from a momentary trance.

"It's all right, then?" asked Vickers.

"Fine," replied Thorpe. "Ah, those rebels will run when they see you coming."

Vickers seemed troubled.

"What's with you, then?" asked Thorpe. "You got this confounded look on that long face of yours."

"They're not all rebels," replied Vickers.

"Have you gone daft?" questioned Thorpe.

"What about Mr. Latham at the tavern or young Richard Davis, the stable boy?" said Vickers. "He's a good lad."

"Come on, then," replied Thorpe. "You should hear yourself. Do you know what you are saying?"

Thorpe knew that some Bostonians remained loyal to King George III, but most supported the rebellious activity that had taken place since the Boston Tea Party. He was surprised to hear Vickers' remarks and wanted to make sure that his fellow soldier understood the consequences of open rebellion against the Crown.

"They broke the King's laws and then they killed his soldiers," explained Thorpe. "They're all rebels. And they'll pay."

"We'll all pay someday," reasoned Vickers.

"Enough of this small talk," interrupted a sergeant, who soon started barking orders: "Attention! Shoulder your firelocks! Rest your firelocks! Order your firelocks! Ground your firelocks!"

The soldiers carefully placed their muskets on the ground.

"Take your ease and get some food in you," instructed the sergeant. "We're going to get busy around here before long and I want you all to be ready."

General William Howe, forty-six years old, a veteran of the French and Indian War who participated in the British victory at Quebec in 1759, examined the landscape before him and the colonial defenses. He peered through his spyglass and saw the redoubt and the breastworks that constituted the main part of the colonial fortification. Several flèches and a long rail fence near the water's edge were defended by other groups of colonists. Nothing extraordinary, he thought, but he noticed that more militia units were reinforcing the defensive positions. Several thousand colonists outnumbered Howe's forces, but the general was convinced, like

General Gage, that part-time provincial militias were no match for the King's professional soldiers. No match at all.

PART ELEVEN

The First Attack

"Don't fire until you see the whites of their eyes."

Dozens of men had fled from the fortifications and the disorganized reinforcements had yet to be properly deployed, but by three o'clock in the afternoon, the colonists appeared as ready as they could be under the circumstances.

The redoubt was filled with armed militiamen under Colonel William Prescott. Captain Josephson's men and other units were positioned behind the breastworks; Captain Thomas Knowlton's men from Connecticut defended the rail fence line; Colonel John Stark's were positioned by the fence and behind a makeshift rock wall near the Mystic River. Armed men were also placed in some of the houses in Charlestown.

Besides Massachusetts and Connecticut, volunteers from New Hampshire filled the ranks. Black militia men, like Peter Salem and Salem Poor, served next to their white comrades. Old men, like seventy-year-old Seth Pomeroy, stood next to teenagers. And professional men, like Boston physician Joseph Warren, shouldered their muskets alongside laborers and farmers. The Massachusetts Provincial Congress elected Warren as its president and appointed him a major general. But the commission had not yet been approved, so Warren joined the ranks at Breed's Hill as a private.

There were over 3,000 colonists on the Charlestown Peninsula and twice as many positioned past the Neck.

"Lots of folks here," exclaimed Hudson as he placed one more shovelful of dirt on the breastworks. "More in these parts than all of Boston, I imagine."

Morgan was so busy working that he didn't even pay attention to Hudson's comments. But after a few more minutes of digging, Morgan paused and rested on his shovel. He was exhausted. The sun was unmerciful. Morgan reached for his canteen. It felt light; it was almost empty. He removed the wooden stopper and drank the last mouthfuls of water.

"You empty, too?" asked Hudson. Morgan nodded as he held his empty canteen upside down. But something startled Morgan.

"What's that?" said Morgan as he stood erect.

"What's what?" replied Hudson.

"Listen," said Morgan.

It was the sound of drums.

"Look!" shouted Morgan as he pointed to the Moulton's Point shoreline, where Gage's soldiers had massed. Drums rolled and Redcoat officers shouted commands as the King's soldiers formed their companies.

"To your arms!" commanded Smith.

The colonists dropped their shovels and rushed to the stacks of muskets. As each man retrieved his weapon, he returned to his place along the defensive fieldworks. Smith worried about how effective his men would be after marching all afternoon and working throughout the night. They had only eaten the food they had carried with them and few had any water left in their canteens. And the sun continued to blaze. But Smith's biggest concern was the lack of ammunition.

General Howe, the senior field officer, had over 2,500 well-trained and experienced soldiers. His light infantry ranks were filled with young, agile men. The grenadiers were big and sturdy and the experienced Royal Marines were trained to fight on land as well as on ships. Howe was confident that he would fulfill General Gage's expectations and crush the rebels.

Howe planned to send companies of light infantry along the Mystic River shoreline and attack Stark's men at the fence and stone barricade. When that position was overrun, the King's troops would turn and attack the rest of the rail fence that Knowlton's men defended. Howe believed that the collapse of those two positions would allow the light infantry to attack the redoubt and breastworks from the rear.

While the shoreline attack was in progress, Howe would command the 23rd Royal Welch Fusiliers and other veteran units in a frontal attack against the redoubt and breastworks. Brigadier General Robert Pigot would lead several regiments on Howe's left; Major John Pitcairn of the Royal Marines was entrusted to protect Pigot's left flank and eliminate the rebel threat in Charlestown.

"There sure are a lot of 'em, sergeant," noted Hudson.

"I didn't think there would be this many," said Goode.

"But we've got them outnumbered," reassured Smith. The sergeant stepped back and ordered: "Look to your arms, men! Make sure those flints are secure!"

The men examined their weapons and cartridge boxes.

"How many cartridges you got?" asked Hudson.

"Not enough," said Morgan.

"Here they come!" shouted Peter Salem.

"Prime and load!" commanded Smith.

Each man with a musket reached for a paper cartridge, bit off the top of it and poured a small amount of gunpowder into the pan. The rest of the cartridge — with its lead ball and remaining gunpowder — was placed in the muzzle and rammed down.

As Morgan returned his ramrod to his musket, he remembered how Jeremiah practiced loading and firing. Yesterday seemed like years ago.

Howe's soldiers advanced in three ranks as the drummers beat out the cadence. The grenadiers of the 23rd Royal Welch Fusiliers looked particularly intimidating. They were bigger than the average British regular and their tall bearskin caps made them seem even taller. As they marched forward, their bayonets shone in the sunlight.

"Those got to be the tallest soldiers I ever saw," remarked Salem

"They're Royal Welch Fusiliers wearing big bearskin hats," explained Smith. "That's why they look so tall. You take off those hats and the tops of their heads don't even reach my chest."

Salem looked incredulously at Smith, who cleared his throat.

"Steady now, lads," cautioned Smith. "Steady."

The first rank of Redcoats was less than one hundred yards away. Their faces could be seen by some of the men.

"Steady," repeated Smith. "Wait for them to get within proper range."

"How close is that, sergeant?" asked Bell with a worrisome tone.

"Their eyes, lad," instructed Smith. "Colonel Prescott said, 'don't fire until you see the whites of their eyes.'"

"That's too close," whispered Bell to himself.

The men waited.

"Look over there!" said Rodgers. "They're attacking Colonel Stark's men at the fence." The men tuned to their left and saw the light infantry advance along the shoreline. The Redcoats were about one hundred feet away when the first volley blasted from Stark's men. Dozens of soldiers fell; many were killed instantaneously. A second militia line stepped forward while the first rank reloaded. Another volley rang out with deadly precision. But the King's soldiers pressed forward.

"If they take that fence, they'll outflank us," explained Morgan to Rodgers.

"I wouldn't worry about that right now," said Hudson as he looked back at the soldiers quickly approaching the breastworks.

The men prepared for Sergeant Smith's command to fire. Bell and Rodgers turned and looked at Smith, who awaited orders from Captain Josephson. Bell looked back at the advancing soldiers and focused on a private with bright blue eyes. They were that close.

"Make ready!" ordered Josephson.

"Make ready!" echoed Smith as he lifted his sword into the air so every man could see the command in case they couldn't hear it. The men fully cocked their muskets.

"Present!" shouted Josephson.

"Present!" repeated Smith as hundreds of men leveled their muskets at the oncoming soldiers.

"Fire!" commanded Josephson.

Hundreds of muskets erupted in an irregular volley of smoke and lead. And then hundreds more fired from the redoubt. Dozens of Redcoats fell to the ground.

"Prime and load," shouted Smith. "Give it to 'em, boys!"

Morgan was one of the first to reload and fire. Moments later, Hudson, Rodgers, and Bell fired into the mass of soldiers. Peter Salem stood on top of the redoubt's corner and fired. Another rank of men stepped forward and fired a volley.

Meanwhile, the Royal Marines were having a difficult time trying to dislodge the militia from the protection of the Charlestown houses. The colonial firepower was so effective that Brigadier General Pigot's left flank was threatened. Immediately, word was sent to the Royal Navy ships to fire upon the town with furnace-heated solid shot. The subsequent artillery barrage set many of the houses on fire, but Pigot halted his attack. Colonial musketry had taken a terrible toll on the attacking units.

By the time the smoke cleared in front of the breastworks, the King's soldiers had already faced about and marched towards Moulton's Point. Dozens of soldiers lay dead or dying on the field.

"They're running," exclaimed Sergeant Smith. "They're running, lads!"

"For now," said Morgan quietly as the rest of the men cheered. But Goode overheard Morgan.

"You don't think they'll attack again, do you?" asked Goode. Morgan said nothing.

"They'll never attack again," said Hadley confidently. "Look at them lying there."

Hudson kneeled and prayed. "O Lord, be not far from me," he said. "Stir up thyself, and awake to my judgment…"

"Even unto my cause, my God and my Lord," finished Morgan.

"Providence is surely with us this day," said Hudson.
"So far," replied Morgan. "We'll see when they come again."
"What makes you so sure they'll come again?" asked Hadley.
"I don't see them getting back in those boats, do you?" replied Morgan.
"That may be so, but I sure hope you're wrong," said Goode.
"Amen," whispered Hudson to himself.

PART TWELVE

A Mother's Prayer

"When is father coming home?"

Elizabeth Morgan slowly entered the kitchen. Rachel was busy stirring soup in a kettle over the fire.

"We'll be eating soon," said Rachel. "Have you completed all of your chores? Minerva's been fed?"

"Yes, mother," replied Elizabeth softly as she lowered her head.

"Now then, what's wrong?" asked Rachel as she walked to her daughter and gently lifted her chin with her right hand. "What is the matter?"

"Father," said Elizabeth.

"What about your father?"

"When will he be coming home?" asked Elizabeth.

"Soon, very soon," explained Rachel.

"And will Jeremiah be with him?"

"Yes," replied Rachel. "Of course he will."

"Are they fighting against the soldiers?"

"I don't know, child."

"Do you think they are well?" asked Elizabeth.

"Here, then," instructed Rachel as she patted the seat of a nearby chair. "Sit down with me."

Rachel and Elizabeth sat next to the fire. She placed her hands on her daughter's shoulders and kissed her forehead. "You are becoming quite a young lady, Elizabeth," noted Rachel. "You're taller than Jeremiah was when he was your age."

"Are you not worried about them, mother?" asked Elizabeth.

"Of course I am, my dear."

"But you don't seem worried."

"I am, but I asked God to watch over them."

Elizabeth paused and stared at her mother.

"But what if He didn't hear you?"

"Then I will ask Him again," smiled Rachel as she held Elizabeth close to her.

PART THIRTEEN

The Second Attack

"We will be victorious!"

Back at the landing area, General Howe was informed that several hundred of his soldiers had been killed or wounded. And a number of men were unaccounted for. Nevertheless, Howe ordered his officers to prepare for another attack.

Thorpe walked over to Vickers, who was kneeling and drinking from his canteen. "You all right, then?" asked Thorpe.

"Yes," said Vickers.

Thorpe noticed a musket ball hole in Vickers' pack.

"Well now, some Provincial had his eye on you," joked Thorpe. "Thank Providence he was aiming at your head."

Vickers wasn't amused. "How can you make sport after what happened?" asked Vickers as he sat down in a patch of tall grass.

"'Tis the only way to get through this bloody madness," replied Thorpe seriously. Vickers nodded and took another drink.

Minutes later, British drummers signaled the soldiers to reform their companies. When they reported to their original company formations, hundreds of empty spaces were evident, especially in the front rank. Vickers and Thorpe had stood shoulder-to-shoulder in the second rank during the initial attack. The non-commissioned officers barked commands for the men in the back ranks to step to the front and fill in the places of the men who were missing. Vickers stepped forward.

The command "Forward…march!" echoed across the Redcoat ranks.

Behind Bunker Hill, Jeremiah and Luke listened as the sound of the drums grew louder. A cart with two dead men was pulled past them. Luke was speechless. He had never seen a dead man before. A flash of fear crossed his face as he thought about his father.

"You think that…" said Luke.

"They're all right," replied Jeremiah.

"Those guns sounded worse than thunder," said Luke.

"We'll be hearing them again," stated Jeremiah.

"Then I guess we should be headin' home," reasoned Luke. He turned away towards the road, but Jeremiah didn't move. "Home, Jeremiah."

Inside the breastworks, the men prepared for the second attack. Sergeant Smith ordered the men to reload. Hudson noticed that Morgan fumbled through his cartridge box before he located a cartridge.

"How many do you need?" asked Hudson.

"Can you spare four?" asked Morgan.

"I only got four," said Hudson.

"And four is all you'll need, me brave fellows," reassured Smith.

As the soldiers advanced, a few random musket shots went off inside the redoubt and along the breastworks.

"Steady, lads," urged Smith. "Hold your fire. Wait for the command. Hold your fire."

When the first rank of Redcoats marched up to where their dead comrades lay, the colonists fired.

"Take 'em!" shouted Smith.

Dozens of soldiers fell. The second rank of men immediately stepped forward on the march and filled the positions of the fallen men. The British troops halted and fired a volley; colonists fell all along the breastworks. A second ragged volley thundered into the Redcoat formation. A loud moan echoed over the battlefield as wounded men on both sides cried out in painful agony. More shots rang out from the redoubt. Separate volleys followed along the breastworks and fence line.

The King's soldiers retreated again.

The sound of muskets hitting the ground behind him startled Morgan. He turned and saw three men running away. Further down the line, a few more men ran towards the safety of Bunker Hill. It was noticeable to everyone that men had fled the battle line. Sergeant Smith didn't want others to follow them, but he hesitated to yell at the remaining men with orders to hold their positions.

"No need to worry, lads," said Smith. "Their empty muskets were of no use anyway."

Goode wasn't convinced. He needed reassurance. "We'll stop them lobsterbacks again, eh, Sergeant?" said Goode.

"That we will," remarked Smith, although his confident expression soon gave way to a concerned look that Morgan noticed.

Morgan, Hudson, and Rodgers rested against the breastworks while Smith searched the cartridge box of a man who had been killed. Bell sat on a large rock and lifted his empty canteen to his lips. He knew that he had taken his last drink before the first attack, but he was so thirsty that the mere motion of drinking was satisfying enough.

Hadley stared at the hundreds of bodies scattered across the battlefield and thought about his cousin, Samuel, who had been killed on Lexington Green. After the first attack was repulsed, Hadley's vengeance had been satisfied. But after the second assault, his rage had been tempered. He could hear the screams of British soldiers writhing in pain on the battlefield. He wondered when all of this would end.

At approximately five p.m., Howe met with his officers. But not all were present.

"I wanted all of my officers here," demanded Howe. "Where are they?"

"Dead, sir," stated one officer from the Royal Marines whose head was bandaged. Howe paused to look at the battlefield strewn with the bodies of the dead and dying.

"Gentlemen, your assessments, please," said Howe.

Some officers suggested that another attack would be disastrous. "Sir, so many have been killed," said an officer from the 47th Regiment. "And we have only so many men."

"These rebels are well armed and supplied," said an officer from the 52nd Regiment. "We should return to Boston and reassess our strategy."

Howe disagreed.

"Are there other voices?" asked Howe. "Speak."

"Sir, fewer firelocks fired along the end of the breastworks on our last attack," said an officer from the 5th Regiment. "They may be running out of powder."

"Quite," said Howe. "And if these Provincials have no powder, they will not stand against us. Our next attack will be successful."

"Sir, is it necessary then for the men to wear packs?" asked an officer from the 23rd Royal Welch Fusiliers.

Howe glanced at Breed's Hill. "Have the men remove their knapsacks and prepare for a third and final assault," ordered Howe. "We will be victorious. Report to your regiments."

The regimental officers returned to their units and passed Howe's orders to the company commanders. Within minutes, every enlisted man was informed that another attack would take place.

"You think we'll take 'em this time?" asked Vickers as he shook off his pack and placed it on the ground. But Thorpe said nothing. A look of worry replaced his usual carefree expression. His dream of military adventure was replaced by the realities and horror of the battlefield.

Corporal Dexter, his right arm in a bloody sling, walked up to Vickers. "How's it be?" asked Dexter.

"Better than you, it seems," replied Vickers. "What happened?"

"That last volley," said Dexter. "A ball cracked me arm above the wrist."

"Sorry, mate," replied Vickers.

"No tears for me, though," said Dexter. "The old sawbones said it would heal proper on its own."

"No sawing it off at the elbow this time, eh?" smiled Vickers.

"No, not this day," remarked Dexter. "But there's a hundred like me over there, a whole regiment of walking wounded. And another regiment of dead."

"So you're out of this next one?" asked Vickers.

"Seems like," said Dexter, who noticed that the usually talkative Thorpe remained unusually quiet as he sat and cleaned his musket. Thorpe looked up at Dexter, but didn't say a word.

"What's with him?" asked Dexter.

"He's not been himself since that last attack," said Vickers.

"Me, either," replied Dexter as he slightly lifted his wounded arm.

PART FOURTEEN

The Final Attack

"We've got to hold this ground!"

A somber message quickly spread through the colonial ranks: Captain Josephson had been killed. One by one, the men along the breastworks began to turn and stand as a cart that carried Josephson's body approached. As it passed by, each man removed his hat.

"His daughter was going to be married next week," said Rodgers.

"And now his wife's a widow because of a small piece of lead," replied Smith. "What a shame."

Morgan thought about what Sergeant Smith said. What if he should die? He imagined Rachel without him. How would she care for the children and the farm by herself? Would she be penalized for being the wife of a rebel if Gage's soldiers won the day?

"William?" said Hudson.

"Huh?" replied Morgan.

"You looked lost there for a moment," said Hudson. Morgan looked at Hudson as if he were about to say something, but the words did not follow. He looked at another cart with several dead militiamen on it and then turned back to his friend.

"If they do attack again and something should happen to me, would you tell Rachel..." instructed Morgan.

"You tell her yourself when you and Jeremiah get back home," interrupted Hudson as he placed his left hand on Morgan's shoulder. Hudson would hear nothing of the sort. Morgan appreciated his friend's optimism. He nodded at Hudson and smiled.

At the first sound of drums, Smith climbed on top of the breastworks. "To your arms!" shouted Smith. "They'll be coming again."

"We've got to hold this ground," replied Hudson.

"And if we hold it, they won't dare to attack again," said Morgan. "They can only sustain so many losses."

"I hope General Gage feels the same way," added Hudson.

Smith walked up and down the line.

"Who is low on cartridges?" asked Smith. Nearly everyone raised his hand. Those who didn't reached in their cartridge boxes and distributed whatever they could spare to those who needed them.

"So what do we do when we run out?" asked Bell.

"I'm already out," quipped Goode, who only had his shovel.

"We *will* run out," said Hudson. "That's for sure."

"But they don't know that," replied Morgan.

"They'll find out soon enough," said Rodgers.

"Every one of Gage's men knows that he is marching into certain death if they keep attacking," explained Morgan. "There'll come a time when they won't stomach another attack."

"Well, it looks like they have the stomach for this one," noted Hudson. "Here they come."

There were fewer soldiers in the third attack, but reinforcements led by General Clinton strengthened the formidable advance. As the sound of the drums increased, the Redcoat formations began concentrating on the redoubt and breastworks. Only light infantry companies remained focused on the fence and the beach defensive positions. Howe planned to keep Stark's men occupied so they could not reinforce his main point of attack.

Howe's soldiers were within one hundred yards of the breastworks; wounded men could be seen in their ranks. Bandages had replaced hats on some men; other soldiers noticeably limped.

"They don't look like they did on their first try," said Morgan.

"And I ain't got as many cartridges as I did on their first try," remarked Hudson.

"What do you have?" asked Morgan.

"One down the barrel and none in the cartridge box," replied Hudson.

The Redcoats were within fifty yards of the fortifications when the commands were given to fire.

"Make ready!" shouted Smith. "Present! Fire!"

Hundreds of muskets erupted. Another large painful sigh was heard in Howe's ranks as men dropped by the dozens. Private Geoffrey Thorpe was among the dead. But the soldiers pressed forward with their muskets leveled.

"Push on!" screamed Vickers as he stepped over Thorpe's body. "Come on, then!"

The British soldiers who had survived the deadly musket volley maintained their disciplined advance.

"Hold steady!" shouted Vickers, who had gained a sense of reckless abandon after his good friend had fallen.

Some colonists who were out of ammunition ran from the fortifications. Smith noticed that one area along the breastworks had few men to defend it.

"Morgan! Will Morgan!" shouted Smith. "I want you to take every other man down to Peter Salem and go reinforce the center of the line. Now! Move!"

Morgan, Salem, and about a dozen others rushed to the undermanned area. They got into position, cocked their muskets, and fired. Smoke filled the air. A few more shots came from random muskets and more Redcoats fell. But most of the colonial muskets were without ammunition. Some of the British soldiers broke from their ranks and ran towards the fortifications. Vickers sensed victory as he raced ahead of the men in his company. A few colonists started throwing rocks and chunks of wood, anything to stop the advancing troops. But nothing would deter the King's soldiers.

In an instant, a dozen British soldiers stormed over the breastworks. And scores more followed. Inside the redoubt, the colonists were no match for trained soldiers with bayonets. The hand-to-hand fighting was brutal. One soldier attempted to stab Hudson, but Morgan clubbed the Redcoat with his empty musket. Goode's shovel could not stop Vickers' bayonet and the Quaker fell to the ground. Isolated musket shots rang out.

The colonial defenses collapsed.

PART FIFTEEN

Young Soldiers

"Don't do it, Jeremiah!"

It was a horrible sight.

Jeremiah and Luke stood by a line of tents at the base of Bunker Hill, where wounded men had been placed. Painful groans could be heard from nearly every tent. "God help me!" shouted a man with a shattered arm. Along the main path, bodies on the ground had been covered with blankets. Two seriously wounded men were carried off a cart.

Thomas Russell, his lower left leg bleeding, limped by using his musket as a crutch. He looked both boys in the eyes with a distant stare and almost started to cry. When he reached the tent, he dropped his musket. Jeremiah stared at his musket while Luke gave Russell a drink of water from a wooden canteen.

"Thank you, lad," said Russell, who grabbed his leg. "Providence may be calling for me, but I'll just donate the leg for now.

"More, sir?" asked Luke.

Russell nodded and Luke handed him the canteen.

"If the fusiliers get here, they won't spare a man," stated Russell. "And that goes for the both of you. Better if you both get out of here."

Russell crawled into the tent.

Jeremiah remained motionless for a few moments and then closed his eyes and spoke softly to himself: "God, provide me with the courage to do what I must do." He picked up a cartridge box and placed it over his shoulder. Then he lifted Russell's musket off the ground. Jeremiah cleared some dirt from the muzzle, removed the ramrod from the weapon, and inserted it down the barrel. "Clean," stated Jeremiah as he returned the ramrod. "Good."

"Don't do it, Jeremiah," warned Luke as he stood up. "Your father will give you a lickin'."

"My father and yours may be dead," reasoned Jeremiah as he half cocked the musket.

"Jeremiah, don't go," pleaded Luke.

"All the men are going," said Jeremiah. He lifted up the flap of the cartridge box and counted the cartridges. Jeremiah glanced at Luke and ran towards the sound of the guns.

"Water," cried Russell. Luke looked around for another canteen and found one on the body of a dead colonist. The canteen was nearly empty, but it would do. Luke watched as Jeremiah rushed into a cloud of gun smoke. As soon as he disappeared, another volley of musketry went off. Luke handed the canteen to Russell and ran after his friend.

PART SIXTEEN

Bayonets Against Fists

"You're heading to certain death!"

The British soldiers were gaining control of the colonial defenses. Out of cartridges, most of the colonists used their empty muskets as clubs. Some threw rocks and others fought with their bare hands. But they were no match for Redcoat bayonets. Hadley and Bell fought side by side until close-range musket fire ended their final stand; Rodgers fell from a bayonet thrust.

An order from Colonel Prescott echoed down the colonial line: "Fall back!"

Sergeant Smith repeated the command: "Fall back!" The entire colonial line began to retreat. Smith noticed that Morgan and Hudson were still fighting and became quickly isolated from the rest of the men. "Will! Joshua!" screamed Smith. "Fall back!"

At that moment, a Royal Welch Fusilier rushed at Hudson. Morgan countered his bayonet thrust with a swing of his musket. Hudson jumped on the rugged Redcoat and dragged him to the ground, where they fought. Morgan clubbed the soldier unconscious and then helped Hudson to his feet. Morgan glanced around and noticed that they were the only men from their militia company left at the breastworks. "Come on, then, back to Bunker Hill," ordered Morgan.

The two ran from their positions as a group of Royal Marines aimed at them with their muskets. An officer yelled: "Make ready! Present! Fire!" Hudson dove for the ground as the muskets fired; Morgan kept on running. Despite the musket volley, no shots hit Morgan. He darted quickly to the right in case other muskets were aimed at him. Moments later, Morgan turned to see where Hudson was, but his friend had vanished from sight.

Inside the redoubt, many of the men had managed to escape thanks to Dr. Joseph Warren and a handful of men who protected them from the advancing Redcoats. But a British volley killed Warren and the rest of the brave militia volunteers.

The fighting at the rail fence and at the makeshift stone wall near the beach was just as intense. Brutal hand-to-hand struggles generated hundreds of casualties as the colonial defenses collapsed. Colonel Stark led his men away from the battered rail fence and reorganized them into a firing line to protect Colonel Prescott's retreating soldiers.

The remnants of Colonel Prescott's militia force on Breed's Hill reformed on the slope of Bunker Hill. The few men with cartridges left reloaded and fired. A small militia group appeared at the crest of Bunker Hill. Jeremiah was with them and they ran quickly to join Prescott's line.

"Whether you've got a round left or not, I want you to raise your firelocks on my command," ordered Prescott. "The more muskets they see, the better."

It was more of a show of force than true firepower, but Prescott wanted the pursuing regulars to think that the colonists were stronger than they were. Jeremiah stood near the end of the line.

On the other side of Bunker Hill, Luke ran into Morgan.

"Mr. Morgan, have you seen my father?" asked Luke. "Have you seen him? Is he all right?"

Morgan placed a comforting hand on Luke's shoulder. Morgan found it difficult to say anything until he realized that Jeremiah was also not around. Morgan turned and looked in every direction. Luke knew Morgan was looking for Jeremiah.

"He took up a musket," said Luke. "Headed back to you."

Joseph Rodgers emerged from a group of wounded. "Will, you're alive," said Rodgers as he pressed his left hand against a bayonet wound in his side. "We're ordered back further." Although Morgan was glad to see his friend had survived the attack, he was more concerned about Jeremiah and Hudson.

"Have you seen my son?" asked Morgan frantically. "And have you seen Joshua Hudson?" Rodgers shook his head.

"Jeremiah!" screamed Morgan as he ran back towards Breed's Hill.

"Will, come back!" shouted Rodgers. "You're heading to certain death!"

Morgan ran along the side of Bunker Hill and saw Prescott's ragged defensive line in the distance. Groups of retreating men blocked his way as he weaved in and out of the chaos. A familiar face emerged from all the rest. Morgan noticed Hudson.

"Joshua, you're alive," smiled Morgan.

"You might…say so," said a winded Hudson as he placed his hands on his knees.

"Jeremiah?" asked Morgan. "Have you seen Jeremiah?"

"I thought he was back at Bunker Hill or on the road home," replied Hudson.

"He was, but he went to our lines," said Morgan

"Luke, too?" asked Hudson.

"No, he's back with the wounded," said Morgan.

"Wounded?" asked Hudson. "Luke's wounded? What happened to him?"

"He's fine," reassured Morgan. "He was comforting the wounded." Hudson gave a sigh of relief, but noticed the worry on Morgan's face.

The roar of approaching Redcoat voices interrupted the men's conversation. "Come on!" ordered Hudson as he pulled Morgan's arm.

"I can't go back," stated Morgan. "I've got to find Jeremiah."

Morgan ran from Hudson towards the last group of retreating militia. "Jeremiah!" shouted Morgan as he searched for his son amidst the last handful of battle-scarred volunteers. He could not imagine his family without Jeremiah, but it seemed that his son was lost. He knew that Rachel would be devastated by his death. And she would hold him responsible for allowing Jeremiah to join the militia.

Another group of colonists came out of the battlefield smoke, mostly Medford men. Jeremiah wasn't with them. Morgan felt his world collapsing. But suddenly a voice rang out from another gunpowder haze: "Father!" It was Jeremiah.

"Jeremiah!" yelled Morgan as he ran to his son. He held his son as if he never wanted him to escape his arms. Hudson approached them. "Maybe this family reunion can wait til later?" said Hudson as he viewed the approaching Redcoats. All three quickly fled the area.

The hastily organized colonial defense at Bunker Hill collapsed quickly. The British maintained their advance as they approached the rise on the hill. A few musket shots by some Connecticut men hit their marks, but the Redcoats kept coming.

The remainder of the various militia units departed the Charlestown peninsula and reformed along the road to Cambridge. However, the British soldiers, exhausted from three attacks, halted their advance at Bunker Hill. They could not have extended their attack beyond the peninsula because the narrow neck was well defended by thousands of additional militiamen. The Battle of Breed's Hill was over. The King's soldiers controlled the entire peninsula from Moulton's Point and Charlestown to Breed's Hill and Bunker Hill.

But it was a costly victory. Of the 2,700 soldiers General Gage ordered into battle under Howe's command, nearly half had been either wounded or killed.

Outside of Cambridge, the veterans of Breed's Hill rested. They filled their canteens, ate, and counted their losses. Nearly 120 colonists were killed and over 300 more were wounded.

"Well, lads, I'm proud of ya," said Sergeant Smith. He looked at Jeremiah. "Proud of you all." Then he faced Luke. "The wounded men give their thanks to you for your help," added Smith. Jeremiah and Luke exchanged smiles.

Smith stood and looked towards the peninsula.

"We'll always remember Captain Josephson," said Smith as he removed his hat. "And Richard Bell. Timothy Goode. Thomas Hadley. God rest their souls."

"And for what?" questioned Rodgers. "We never held the hills."

"Listen to me, Joseph," said Smith. "The best soldiers in the world had to make three attacks before they pushed us back. Us! Look at *us*! Look at who we are: Farmers and shopkeepers, schoolteachers and dock workers. Tavern workers and teamsters. Gage paid a terrible price for all of that because of what Bell and the rest of those brave lads did on this day."

"Gage lost many a good man today," said Morgan.

"Just to take these hills," replied Hudson.

"Our thirteen colonies are filled with such hills," stated Morgan. He put his arm around Jeremiah.

PART SEVENTEEN

A Costly Victory

"There is something about these people."

At his headquarters, General Gage stood before his seated officers. Minutes passed before anything was said.

"The third attack brought victory," said General Clinton.

"Victory?" questioned Gage. "Over one thousand of our men, nearly one hundred of our officers, killed or wounded."

General Howe lowered his head. "There was a moment that we never felt before," said Howe. "And all those men dead and at the hands of provincials."

"Provincials, you call them?" replied Gage. "Mere provincials, some would say."

Howe looked up. "Sir?" questioned Howe.

"There is something about these people," said Gage as if he were talking to himself. "Their will, their resolve. I am not sure what it is, but it is something that we have never witnessed before."

Clinton stood. "We have the might on land and at sea to suppress this rebellion," said Clinton.

"Yes, I'm sure," said Gage in a soft voice. Gage walked towards a window. "Thank you, gentlemen."

His officers left the room. Gage remained standing at the window for quite some time. "But there is something about these people," he thought.

Epilogue

During the summer of 1775, the first Continental Army troops arrived outside of Boston: riflemen from Pennsylvania, Virginia, and Maryland. General George Washington, the new commander-in-chief of the army, arrived in July. In September, Gage was recalled to Great Britain; General Howe replaced him.

The Continental and British armies faced each other across the harbor during the winter months. Neither side attacked the other. Only isolated rifle shots from colonial marksmen suggested that an armed military struggle had been underway for months.

But the situation changed drastically in March when dozens of artillery pieces captured at Fort Ticonderoga were placed around the hills outside of Boston. The British evacuated the city on March 17, 1776.

In July, the rebellious colonies declared themselves free and independent states. However, the British returned and invaded the newly-formed United States of America. The war raged on until 1783 when the Treaty of Paris officially ended the war and Great Britain recognized the United States as a nation of the world.

William Morgan joined the Continental Army as a member of the 10th Massachusetts Regiment. He was elected a captain in 1777 and served during the Saratoga Campaign in which American forces were victorious over General Burgoyne, one of the high-ranking officers who served under General Gage during the Battle of Bunker Hill. Burgoyne's surrender prompted France to recognize the United States and the nation came to the new republic's aid. Morgan survived the war and returned home to his family.

Jeremiah Morgan joined the Continental Army in 1778 on his sixteenth birthday. He served in the Southern campaign under General Nathaniel Greene and witnessed the surrender of General Cornwallis at Yorktown. At the end of the war, he returned home for a while and then traveled to Tennessee, where he established a home, married, and became an officer in the Lawrence County militia. Among his friends was the celebrated frontiersman David Crockett.

Joshua and Luke Hudson sold their farm and moved to Rhode Island. Joshua Hudson joined the Continental Army and also served in the Southern Campaign. He fought at the Battle of Guilford Courthouse in North Carolina on March 17, 1781. During the battle, a gunshot shattered his left arm. A battlefield surgeon amputated his arm, but Hudson did not survive.

When Luke was informed of his father's death, he left Rhode Island and joined the crew of a merchant ship. He circumnavigated the earth twice and learned to speak several languages. Luke returned to Rhode Island, where he became a teacher. He married and started a family. He named his first son Jeremiah.

William Morgan and his family learn that the militia has been called to arms.

William Morgan and his loyal friend, Joshua Hudson.

Luke Hudson and Jeremiah Morgan want to be a part of the militia.

William Morgan and Joshua Hudson look towards Boston.

The colonists discuss the possibility of reconciliation with the Crown.

Joshua Hudson and William Morgan express concern for their families.

The British advance towards the colonial defenses.

Farmers and shopkeepers prepare to fight the King's soldiers.

The colonists fire their first deadly volley.

The British soldiers suffer numerous casualties.

The British soldiers finally overrun the colonial defenses.

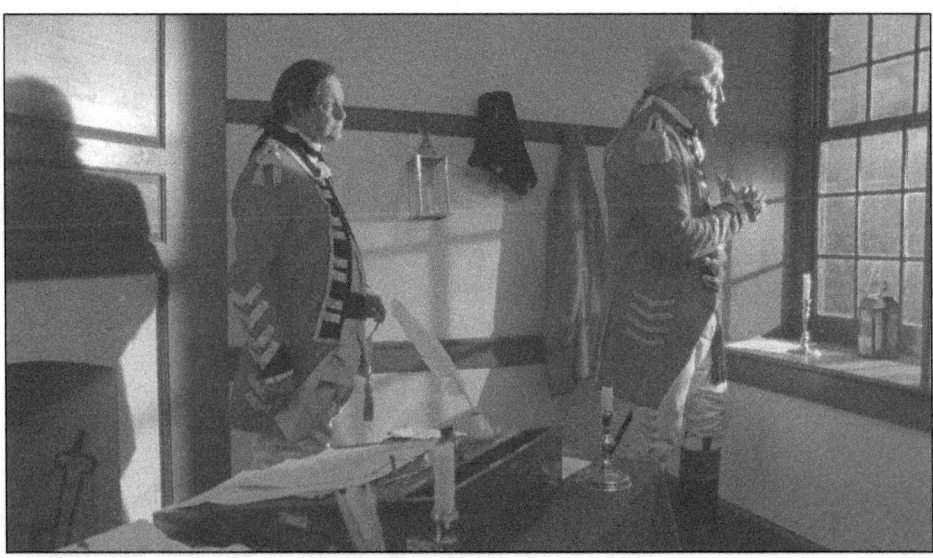
General Gage (right) and General Clinton express concern over their costly victory.

The Battle of Bunker Hill producer-director Tony Malanowski.

APPENDIX A

Causes of the American Revolution

The Battle of Bunker Hill on June 17, 1775, was the first major battle of the American Revolution. It followed the outbreak of hostilities between British soldiers and colonists at Lexington and Concord, Massachusetts, on April 19, 1775.

The fighting in Massachusetts was the result of tensions that had developed between the mother country and colonial America since 1763, when Great Britain won the French and Indian War. As a result of the Treaty of Paris, which officially ended the conflict, France gave up what is now Canada and lands east of the Mississippi River. But Great Britain generated a large war debt as a result of the war with France. Furthermore, King George III's nation now had to maintain an administrative and military presence in the newly acquired lands.

In order to pay off some of the war debts and to finance the defense of the new territories, Great Britain expected its American colonies to contribute to the costs. The British Parliament passed a series of laws that taxed and regulated the colonists. But the colonists had no say in the laws and some exclaimed that there shall be "no taxation without representation" in Parliament.

Starting in 1763, each new law passed by Parliament increased the tensions between Great Britain and the American colonies. Twelve years later, the Revolutionary War began.

Timeline

1763: *Proclamation of 1763*

This law was designed to protect colonial settlers from Indian attacks on the frontier by ordering them to move east of the Appalachian Mountains. Frontier families didn't like to be told where they could or could not live.

1764: *Sugar Act*

This law placed taxes on sugar, molasses, and other products imported from outside the British empire. Although the law reduced the tax amounts, it was strictly enforced by British officials.

1765: *Stamp Act*

This law placed a direct tax on various items — from newspapers and legal documents to playing cards and dice. A Royal stamp indicated the amount of the tax on each item. The colonists protested the law with a Stamp Act Congress, a boycott of British goods, and acts of violence. The law was repealed in 1766.

1765: *Quartering Act*

This law required that British soldiers be housed in barracks and public houses provided by the colonies.

1766: *Declaratory Act*

Parliament reasserted its right of "full power and authority" over the colonies following the repeal of the Stamp Act.

1767: *Townshend Acts*

This law placed taxes on various imports like glass, lead, paper, paint, and tea. A successful boycott eventually eliminated all of the taxes by 1770, except the one on tea.

1770: *Boston Massacre*

An outbreak of hostilities between colonists and British soldiers erupted in Boston on March 5, 1770. Five colonists were shot and killed. Other colonists were wounded.

1773: *Tea Act*

This law granted a monopoly to the British East India Company to sell tea in the colonies.

1773: *Boston Tea Party*

A colonial revolt in Boston Harbor on December 16, 1773, that resulted in the destruction of 342 chests of tea.

1774: *Intolerable Acts*
A series of measures passed by Parliament designed to punish Boston for the Tea Party. These Coercive Acts closed Boston Harbor to trade and placed restrictions on town meetings, among other punitive acts.

1774: *First Continental Congress*
A meeting in Philadelphia in which representatives from twelve of the thirteen colonies (Georgia did not send representatives) discussed the problematic Intolerable Acts.

1775: *Lexington and Concord*
An outbreak of fighting between British soldiers and armed colonists in Massachusetts which resulted in hundreds of casualties.

1775: *Second Continental Congress*
A meeting in Philadelphia in which representatives from all thirteen colonies discussed British actions and laws. The Second Continental Congress created a Continental Army and appointed George Washington as its commander. It declared independence from Great Britain in 1776.

JUNE 17, 1775: *The Battle of Bunker Hill*

APPENDIX B

Historical Notes

Approximately 2,500 colonists participated in the Battle of Bunker Hill. Commanded by General Israel Putnam, the colonists withheld two major assaults by the British before yielding their defensive positions. Nearly 120 were killed and over 300 were wounded. Another thirty were captured. Most of the casualties came during the final assault and the subsequent retreat.

Although a British victory, General Thomas Gage's ranks were decimated. According to one account, of the approximate 2,700 soldiers in General William Howe's attacks, 207 enlisted men and nineteen officers were killed. Another 766 enlisted men and sixty-two officers were wounded. General Henry Clinton noted: "A few more such victories would have shortly put an end to British dominion in America."

George Washington, who was appointed commander of the Continental Army on June 15, 1775, two days before the battle, arrived in Cambridge on July 2. One year later, the Continental Congress voted for independence.

Several days after General Gage's report on the battle reached Parliament, he was dismissed from command and replaced by General Howe, who served until October 1777, when he submitted his resignation following the disastrous Saratoga Campaign. Parliament accepted his resignation in the spring of 1778.

The War for American Independence continued until the Treaty of Paris formally ended the conflict on September 3, 1783.

On June 17, 1825, the fiftieth anniversary of the battle, a cornerstone was laid for the Battle of Bunker Hill Monument. Periodic construction work on the granite obelisk continued until July 23, 1842, when the capstone was placed atop the structure. On June 17, 1843, the monument, which stands 221 feet tall, was dedicated during a public ceremony. Today, the Bunker Hill Monument is operated by the National Park Service.

APPENDIX C

Cast and Crew

Light a Candle Films presents A Little Warsaw Production
The Battle of Bunker Hill
2009

Produced and Directed by	Tony Malanowski
Associate Producers	William Chemerka
	Kevin Reem
1st Assistant Director	Heinrich Montgomery
2nd Assistant Director	Ben Mario
2nd Unit Director/Battle Choreographer	William Chemerka
Directors of Photography	Peter Mullett
	Dan Donley
1st Assistant Cameraman	Daniel Poole
Assistant Cameramen	Matt Holder
	Mike Krebs
Additional Cameramen	David Ellis
	Kevin Reem
	Tony Malanowski
	Stephanie Safka
Clapper/Loader	Bobby Ogden
Image Camera Work	Alice Starr Leggin
Image Camera Operators	Alison Malanowski
	Melissa Malanowski
Mini DV/EPK Cameraman	Daniel Poole
Interview Videographer	Edward Martin Productions
	Ed Hobelman
Unit Photographer	Jennifer Rouse
Music by	William Stromberg
	John Morgan
Additional Orchestration	Anna Bonn
Screenplay by	William Chemerka
Original Story by	Tony Malanowski

Script Supervisor	Carrie Marks
Sound Mixers	Rick Angelella
	Bruce Litecky
Boom Operators	Mark Mariaca
	Bob Mellor
	Robert Esposito
Lighting by	Serious Grip and Electric
	Location Lighting Ltd.
Best Boy	Billy Pratt
Gaffers	Rob Mabin
	Jeff Herberger
	Chu Kinyama
	Butch Van Putt
Edited by	Tony Malanowski
Assistant Editor	Skip Garrett
Sound Editing/Design by	Desolation Row Sound Studios
Assistant Sound Editor	Robert Zimmerman
Music Editor	James W. Hale
ADR/Foley Recording	Bastille Productions, Inc.
	Jerry Houser
Sound Mix by	Audio Mechanics
Audio Mixer	John Polito
Sound Effects by	Kevin Reem
	Sounddogs.com
	Bastille Productions, Inc.
	Frank Allison Coe
Visual Effects by	Daniel Leland Baldwin
C.G. Artist	James Ludwig
Historical Portraits by	Don Troiani
Make Up/Hair	Jennifer Rouse
Secondary Make Up	Yvonne Darell
	Tina Waters
Special Effects by	No Joke, Inc.
	Jeffrey Cox
Set Construction by	Mark Redfield
	Wayne Shipley
	Clay Supensky
	Matt Holder
	Conway Gainesford
Horse Provided by	West End Farm

Wrangler	Heather Stubanas
Unit Production Manager	Deborah Chemerka
Unit Publicist	Katie Gregg
Production Accountant	Ali Paskun
Production Secretary	Dario Ardujinas
On-Line Editor	Brett Truett
	ENCORE, HOLLYWOOD
TeleCine Colorists	Keith Roddy
	George Koran
	Tom Sartori
	Greg Kautz
Assistant Operator	Ignacio Sanchez
Stock Footage/Images	Getty Images
	The Image Bank
	Kevin Hershberger
	LionHeart Film Works, L.L.C.
	National Archives
	Library of Congress
	Ronald Reagan Presidential Library
	FDR Presidential Library
	Woodrow Wilson Presidential Library
Location Correspondent	Russ Green
Locations	Howell Living History Farm
	Pete Watson
	Gary Houghton
	Old Barracks Museum
	Art Decorating Company
	Action Cat Studios
Laboratory Services	Cinetech
	ColorLab
	DuArt
	FotoKem
Catering by	The Sneaky Caterer
Costumes by	Druid's Oak
	3 Horse Hill
	Jeff Finegan
	Rick Bilz
Props by	Avalon Forge
	C.W. Enterprises/Earl Becker
	Historic Military Services

Courier Service .... Reels on Wheels
Insurance by .... Insurance West Corporation
Premium Financial Specialists of Ca., Inc.

CAST

William Morgan	Mark Redfield
Joshua Hudson	Michael Mack
Jeremiah Morgan	Christopher Hampson
Luke Hudson	Brandon Thompson
Rachel Morgan	Sandy O'Brien
Elizabeth Morgan	Miranda Savage
Sgt. Matthew Smith	David Emerson
General Thomas Gage	Ken Siegel
General Henry Clinton	Don F. Beale
Thomas Russell	Dana Joel Bogdanski
Bradley Quinn	John Pagano
Joseph Rodgers	Chuck Speierl
Geoffrey Thorpe (Brit. #1)	Paul Astle
Errol Vickers (Brit. #2)	Nigel Eastwood
Timothy Goode	Ian Haight-Ashton
Richard Bell	Rick Bilz
Orderly	Jason Meyer
Featured Historians	Dr. Gregory J.W. Urwin
	Richard Patterson
	William Chemerka
Candle Kid #1	Melissa Malanowski
Narration by	David Prince

APPENDIX D

The Battle of Bunker Hill

DVD Docudrama

SCENE SELECTIONS:
1. Preview/Introduction
2. The Seeds of Revolution
3. Main Titles/Feed the Chickens
4. Joseph Rodgers/The Road to Boston
5. "I'm glad we're free."
6. "This is just beginning..."
7. Morning Barrage
8. Gage's Plan
9. First Assault/Battlefield Prayer
10. Behind the Lines/Second Assault
11. "All the men are going."/Final Assault
12. "Something about these people..."/End Credits

Historical Perspective

SCENE SELECTIONS:
1. Birth of Rebellion
2. The Players
3. Colonial Farm Life
4. Faith in the Colonies
5. General Gage
6. Defenses
7. "Don't Fire Until..."
8. Black Patriots
9. Tactics
10. The Battle
11. Colonial Sacrifice

APPENDIX E

The Battle of Bunker Hill

DVD Special Features

Digitally Mastered Audio and Anamorphic Video
16 x 9 Widescreen Presentation

Audio: English 5.1 (Dolby Digital) & English 2.0 (Dolby Surround)

Scene Selections

Docudrama: *The Battle of Bunker Hill*
60-minute narrative creation with Historical Commentary

Historical Perspective
30-minute analysis of the Colonial Revolution in 11 segments

Behind the Scenes Featurette: "On the Battlements at Dawn"
A 21-minute look at the Making of *The Battle of Bunker Hill* with Producer/Director Tony Malanowski

Production Overview with star Michael Mack and Interviews with other Cast Members

Great Presidential Moments: The full Farewell Address of President Ronald Wilson Reagan from 1989

Deleted Scene

Trailer

Still Gallery

Bear Manor Media

Classic Cinema.
Timeless TV.
Retro Radio.
WWW.BEARMANORMEDIA.COM

www.ingramcontent.com/pod-product-compliance
Lightning Source LLC
Chambersburg PA
CBHW071626170426
43195CB00038B/2145